Colonization after Emancipation

Colonization after Emancipation

Lincoln and the Movement for Black Resettlement

Phillip W. Magness and Sebastian N. Page

University of Missouri Press
Columbia

University of Missouri Press, Columbia, Missouri 65211
Printed and bound in the United States of America

First paperback printing, 2018

Cataloging-in-Publication data available from the Library of Congress
ISBN 978-0-8262-2149-0 (paperback : alk. paper)

∞™ This paper meets the requirements of the
American National Standard for Permanence of Paper
for Printed Library Materials, Z39.48, 1984.

Typefaces: Adobe Garamond and Bodoni

Contents

Preface

As unlikely as it may seem in retrospect given the present study it produced, this inquiry began as a simple quest to locate an elusive document from Abraham Lincoln's presidency. On June 13, 1863, an agent bearing credentials from the British government sat with Lincoln for a highly secretive interview at the White House. Following a brief discussion of the agent's dealings with a member of the cabinet, the president handed his guest an order drafted by James Mitchell, the government's commissioner of emigration, and bearing Lincoln's own signature. The document outlined a proposal submitted by the agent, himself a representative of a large landholding corporation in the colony of British Honduras, or modern-day Belize. He sought to transport the newly emancipated slaves of the United States to a tract of his company's land. There they would be provided with acreage, dwellings, and tools to begin life anew as free agricultural laborers under the supervision of the British government.

Then the British agent apparently marched off into history, authorization in hand, leaving few indications that he ever acted on its provisions. The American records contained only a second-generation secretary's copy of the paper, neatly tucked away into an obscure file at the Department of the Interior unseen by most historians. This document sparked a corollary discussion of the West Indies scheme in a 2008 article about Lincoln's colonization policies by one of the authors. Still, its own story lingered in mystery and prompted a subsequent search for the original in Lincoln's pen.

This quest led us to the United Kingdom by way of historical dispatches from the British Legation in Washington, D.C., where the agent from Belize filed a report of his business. A succession of document discoveries in the British and American National Archives revealed that the 1863 meeting was part of a much larger colonization project, unknown to this day, wherein the American and British governments sought to populate the West Indies with ex-slaves from the United States. Equally startling, this project occurred in the latter years of Lincoln's presidency when it is commonly believed that he moved away from colonization in favor of his better-known policies to secure the rights and futures of the freedmen in the United States. In short, this elusive document provided both an opportunity to write an unexplored chapter of Lincoln's presidency and an occasion to reexamine the role that colonization played in his efforts to eradicate slavery and his Emancipation Proclamation of January 1, 1863.

The project itself presented a tough shell to crack. Its participants, including Lincoln, left a meager trail of evidence, incomplete from any single holding and scattered across both sides of the Atlantic. The pursuit took us through the interdepartmental memoranda of the British Foreign and Colonial Offices and the American consular records of Belize and Demerara, British Guiana. It led us to the Library of Congress, where a smudged date further obscured our search by way of a misfiled document hiding in plain sight amidst the well known and widely researched Abraham Lincoln manuscript section. We chased the program's American administrator, James Mitchell, to his postwar career as an educator in rural Carroll County, Georgia. Utilizing an extensive assemblage of letters, pamphlets, and newspaper articles, we reconstructed the course of a previously unknown fact-finding mission in which a group of African American abolitionists traveled to Central America to investigate the proposed colony site on behalf of the U.S. Emigration Office.

Ironically, we were unable to accomplish the initial goal of locating the original June 13, 1863, order in Lincoln's handwriting. Though we located a first-generation copy that was filed at the British Legation, the original's whereabouts remain unknown. It was apparently carried off to Belize by its recipient, whereas the primary American copy disappeared into the lost files of the Emigration Office, last seen in Mitchell's possession shortly before his death in 1903. The search bore many other fruits though, primary among them the untold story of Lincoln's last major attempt to colonize the freed slaves abroad.

The remainder of this work provides an account of the Belize project and related efforts to find a home for the freedmen in the Caribbean and Central America. Without exposing the reader to a premature revelation of this story, it is appropriate to attempt an answer at one question it naturally provokes, to wit: why has the attempted colonization of the West Indies with freed slaves from the United States escaped almost all historical attention?

We find no simple answer to this question, except to say that it is a product of events surrounding the scheme's design, attempted implementation, and eventual collapse. Most preparations, including Lincoln's own involvement, occurred well out of the public spotlight and are known to us only through the occasional decision of other involved parties to record them in writing.

The degraded condition of the Emigration Office records was a primary obstacle and bears note. This agency, tasked with administering the American components of the project, also became a cause of its demise when a rancorous bureaucratic fight erupted over the control of its budget. The feud took its toll on the project's records as its principal agents repeatedly relocated their files, intentionally withheld key documents from one another, and dueled for control over tasks related to their administration. Untold dozens of relevant papers disappeared with the fight's primary participants, Mitchell and Interior Secretary John P. Usher. Mitchell undoubtedly carried many away as he moved his files beyond Usher's reach in 1864 and likely retained them in his extensive personal library until his death. Most of these potentially valuable files dispersed among his heirs, their present whereabouts unknown.

We set out to reconstruct the Emigration Office records by using the somewhat chaotic files that survived in the Interior Department's possession as a starting point. From there we identified other records through copies in the British Foreign and Colonial Offices, and through references in surviving letters and contracts. A combination of congressional records, period newspaper reports, and later reminiscences allowed us a glimpse at many of the Emigration Office's otherwise unrecorded activities, including a little-known investigative expedition that it sent to a proposed colony site in August 1863.

The British records provided additional challenges. The project involved two distinct offices of the Palmerston government with policy priorities that did not always coincide. Though the project generated no numerical shortage of records at the British end, they arrived with the inconsistency one might expect from a remote colonial outpost on the empire's frontier. London's negotiations with Washington produced hundreds of pages about the scheme, though its eventual abandonment by the Colonial Office left only a few scant notes in obscure colonial files. In a few instances, only informed conjecture suffices to explain a sudden turn of events by taking notice of its subsequent results.

The irregularity of reliable records, combined with the project's complex participatory arrangements, deflected attention from its story. In the infrequent instances where historians happened upon evidence of the project's existence, most quickly left its trail after encountering a misleading dead end. A multitude of emerging theories about Lincoln's thoughts on colonization, as well as race and slavery in general, further reduced the project's visibility to historians. The attempted colonization of the British West Indies introduces new complications and greater uncertainty to our understanding of Lincoln's better-known policies, such as the Emancipation Proclamation. Combined, these factors have offered little enticement for historians to investigate the associated projects further. To the contrary, the records problem surrounding the schemes openly encouraged their neglect for over a century.

The deciphering of Lincoln's final and least-known push for colonization opens many new and unexpected questions that will likely benefit from the input of the academy and the history enthusiast alike. How do the attempted freedmen's settlements in Belize and other Caribbean locales affect our understanding of colonization, both as a priority for Lincoln and as a policy of the United States government? What was the project's relationship to the Emancipation Proclamation, and how did these two policies interact in Lincoln's mind? What does it say about Britain's views of American slavery or the international response to the early stages of its abolition? What does it tell us about Lincoln's thought process, and the evolution of his views on race, slavery, and equality?

The authors make no claim of resolving these questions only initiating a dialogue that may eventually produce a fuller understanding of Lincoln's comprehension of the issues before him. To this end, we posit several interpretations of our own and examine them within the context of others. As with the story of the British colonization project itself, the questions it raises about Abraham Lincoln are replete with mystery, provocative in their own right, and meritorious of the continued interest that has attracted so many to the remarkable yet enigmatic life of the sixteenth president.

Acknowledgments

We would like to extend our acknowledgment and gratitude to the many individuals who assisted us in our research and provided the support necessary to make this project a reality. First, we would like to thank Jack Dorsey of Mt. Zion, Georgia, for his invaluable assistance with the location of biographical material on Rev. James Mitchell. Dorsey is a local historian and retired educator from the Carroll County School District, the successor institution to a school system founded by Mitchell after his service as Abraham Lincoln's Emigration Commissioner. He is currently the director of the Mt. Zion Community Center.

We also extend our many thanks to Doctors Jay Sexton and Richard Carwardine of the University of Oxford, Adam Tate of Clayton State University, and Catherine Rudder of George Mason University, each of whom provided many helpful suggestions as readers during the development of this manuscript. We further extend our gratitude to Mark Borgiasz and Laura Domyan, who assisted with the editing of source materials and the final preparation of this manuscript for publication.

We would also like to thank the Arts and Humanities Research Council (UK), Peter Parish Memorial Fund, and Corpus Christi College, Oxford, for the funding and bursaries provided to one of the authors, and to the School of Public Policy, George Mason University, which provided a travel grant to assist with the development of this research.

Colonization after Emancipation

Chapter 1

The Curious Politics of Colonization

"Without being an enthusiast, Lincoln was a firm believer in colonization." This was the assessment given to him by presidential secretaries John Nicolay and John Hay in a duly celebrated 1890 biography of their late employer.[1] The colonization of freed slaves, to either Africa or the tropics of Central America and the Caribbean, featured prominently in Abraham Lincoln's formative beliefs on race and slavery. Enabled by a $600,000 appropriation from Congress, Lincoln aggressively pursued the policy in the early part of his presidency.

Lincoln was by no means the first president to advocate colonization. The idea dated to the revolutionary period, when many of the nation's founding fathers grappled with the troublesome place of slavery in a country ostensibly founded on the concept of natural equality as expressed in the Declaration of Independence. Writers from Thomas Jefferson to Alexis de Tocqueville openly expressed vexation over the multiracial future of the North American continent should emancipation ever come. Many leading political figures, Jefferson among them, turned to colonization as a corollary to emancipation. Other early colonizationists included such notable personalities as James Madison, Daniel Webster, Henry Clay, John Randolph of Roanoke, Francis Scott Key, and Bushrod Washington, nephew of the first president.

A variety of motives—political, economic and humanitarian—drove these men to advocate the separation of the races, imbuing the movement with an ambiguous *raison d'être* that confounded contemporaries no less than it does scholars today. It received an institutional face in 1816 with the founding of the American Colonization Society (ACS) whose official policy of removing consenting free blacks, dating from 1822, to its West African progeny, Liberia, gave rise to vastly differing interpretations.

The core of the movement was always self-styled moderates, particularly of the border slave states and lower North, who were quietly looking to ease the processes of gradual emancipation or individual manumissions by offering the critical *quid pro quo* of the expatriation of the African Americans thus freed. This would remove not only what most agreed was both a social and political evil, but also one of the stumbling blocks to conservative antislavery. The mainstream colonizationist rationale was an ambivalent one, best viewed through the lens of Enlightenment environmentalism, even into the nineteenth century. According to its misguided philanthropy, the same freedman population whose very presence inflicted only misery upon both black and white in America (due to the explosive mixture of a 'superior' and an 'inferior' race) could better itself once placed in Africa and bring Christianity and republicanism to that continent.

Not that this middling position satisfied all. Early federal sponsorship of the ACS in its labors of resettling 'recaptives,' the rescued victims of the illegal transatlantic slave trade, came under scrutiny as soon as Andrew Jackson came into office, and although it had many prominent friends, bills for U.S. government assistance in other aspects of its work would henceforth fail. Slaveholders of the lower South, who had shown some initial interest in removing the already free blacks alone, had quickly wised up to the slippery implications of the ACS's definition of "free people of color." From the 1830s their objections were backed by nascent proslavery theory, which upheld the benefits of the institution for all involved. The more painful attack on the movement though, emerging around the same time, came from the other wing, as immediatist abolitionists demanded universal emancipation without conditions attached and decried the justification of racial prejudice which underpinned colonization.

The movement survived due to some disciplined management at the society headquarters and thanks to the existence of state auxiliary organizations which had a freer hand in their work and self-presentation, but they were painful years nonetheless. One of the interesting outcomes of the sectional tension of the late 1840s and 1850s, however, was the countervailing drive for political moderation that it produced in the broad middle of the political spectrum, leading to a resurgence of interest in colonization with its appealing flavor of the apparent unanimity of idealized earlier times.

It is questionable, however, how much the ACS itself benefited politically from this. While it enjoyed increased donations, testamentary bequests of slaves for manumission on condition of removal, and a great deal of lip service, its dominant clerical and humanitarian element was still cautious about venturing into politics. Many of the key proponents of this second wave of colonization were midwesterners rather than easterners of either section, and, frequently backed by the proscriptive race legislation on their states' books, they were arguably a lot more interested in the deportationist side of the scheme, and its racial implications for the U.S., than the civilizing ones for 'benighted' Africa. Indeed, Liberia was out of favor for the geostrategic, closer prize of Central America, which also appealed more to those African Americans who had, given the grim circumstances of the decade, reopened the emigration debate in the 1850s to give greater consideration to a solution that most blacks had rejected, as a denial of their birthright, since the society's formation.

It was in this context that Lincoln inherited the colonization mantle during the formative years of his political career, most notably through the influence of his early political hero Henry Clay and the Whig Party. He advocated the concept as an Illinois legislator, and participated in the Illinois Colonization Society.[2] In 1857 Lincoln declared the "separation of the races" to be the "only perfect preventive of amalgamation," noting that "[s]uch separation, if ever effected at all, must be effected by colonization."[3] He reiterated this stance a year later in one of his most notorious statements from the famous debates with Stephen Douglas during their U.S. Senate campaigns:

> I will say then that I am not, nor ever have been in favor of bringing about in any way the social and political equality of the white and black races,—that I am not nor ever have been in favor of making voters or jurors of negroes, nor of qualifying them to hold office, nor to intermarry with white people; and I will say in addition to this that there is a physical difference between the white and black races which I believe will for ever forbid the two races living together on terms of social and political equality.[4]

This embrace of colonization underwent little material change between 1858 and his election to the presidency. Even before the first shots were fired at Fort Sumter, Lincoln directed Elisha O. Crosby, his newly appointed minister to Guatemala, to investigate the prospects of colonization in Central America.[5]

In his first year in office Lincoln called upon Congress to fund a larger colonization program. Notably, he forged a direct link between this proposal and the earliest forerunner of emancipation, the Confiscation Act of 1861, which permitted the Union army to seize property, including slaves, used in support of the rebellion. By this act, Lincoln declared, the "legal claims of certain persons to the labor and service of certain other persons have become forfeited." He called on Congress to provide "that such persons, on such acceptance by the general government, be at once deemed free." It was but a natural extension of this process that "steps be taken for colonizing" these freedmen "at some place, or places, in a climate congenial to them," and that appropriations be made to acquire territories for that purpose.[6] Congress obliged Lincoln's request, providing the $600,000 colonization fund, $100,000 of which was to be specifically dedicated to the black residents of the District of Columbia.[7]

Though authorized amidst unprecedented wartime expenditures amounting to hundreds of millions of dollars, the colonization fund was no inconsequential side project. To add some perspective, the entire federal budget for the previous year had barely topped $60 million. Beginning on July 16, 1862, the day the appropriation went into effect, Lincoln's personal attention turned to colonization. He established an Emigration Office in the Department of the Interior to administer his colonization policies, directed the State Department to begin negotiations for the acquisition of suitable territories, and pled the scheme's merits before a delegation of free black residents of the District of Columbia. The president also promoted it publicly and ensured his fledgling antislavery strategy contained provisions for the resettlement of blacks abroad. Colonization would serve as an enticement to the slave states that remained in the Union should they enact policies of compensated emancipation. His preliminary Emancipation Proclamation, announced in September 1862, also pledged to "colonize persons of African descent, with their consent, upon this continent, or elsewhere."[8]

From the summer through December 1862, colonization was a recurring topic within the administration's inner circles, where it spawned the earliest attempts of the U.S. government to put the $600,000 fund to use. Two colonization "experiments" initiated during these months have received extensive attention from historians since the time of Hay and Nicolay. The first, a contract to purchase land from a private investor in the Chiriquí region of Panama, began in September and fell through a few months later amidst objections from the British and several Latin American governments. The second, also initiated by contract in December 1862, consisted of an attempt to settle the Île à Vache off the coast of Haiti. The Haitian colony actually received about 450 emigrants before it collapsed a year later, though it proved a disaster from the outset. The contract entrusted the colony to an unscrupulous speculator who squandered the money and left the island without supplies, leading to its abandonment and the subsequent rescue of its starving inhabitants by the United States Navy in 1864.[9]

Here ends the standard account of President Lincoln's venture into colonization, as Hay and Nicolay wrote that the Chiriquí and Île à Vache projects were the only two schemes that "commended themselves to the special attention of the President." In fact, this most curious and controversial component of Lincoln's antislavery policy, the subject of public proclamations and intense private deliberations before the cabinet alike, seems to all but vanish from the standard historical narrative with the ringing in of the New Year in 1863. Henry J. Raymond, one of the first notable Lincoln biographers, gave a similar assessment in 1865 by noting that "[n]o further experiments were made in the matter of colonization" beyond these two attempts.[10] Most historians since Raymond have reached similar conclusions and left the matter with Hay and Nicolay's description, only filling in the remaining details of the two projects. Lincoln's colonization program thus seems to have amounted to a brief flirtation with the policy in the latter half of 1862, the only attempts in pursuit of which ended in embarrassment or stillbirth. From there it is thought he marched forward toward emancipation as a stand-alone policy, the colonizationist inclinations of his youth and his early presidency having been set aside as unworkable, if not willfully abandoned.

It may be duly noted that colonization's apparent wane beyond the two schemes initiated in late 1862 comports well with the notion of the Civil War as an evolutionary narrative on race. Colonization strikes the modern reader as an artifact exemplar, a relic eternally chained to the historical circumstances that produced it and seldom ever a viable strain of policy in its own right. The logistics of transportation alone made the proposition inherently unworkable, as many of its advocates discovered only after trial and error. As a policy, it strays widely from the evolutionary course of race relations over time, both as a pattern of its own, and as the modern reader knows, from the reflection and hindsight offered by the Civil Rights movement.

Nor does colonization provide an easy fit with the Civil War in memory. By its nature, the policy was burdened by the technical complexities of its execution and, thus, detached from any sweeping sense of philosophical significance. Colonization defies the conclusiveness granted to the slavery narrative by the final act of emancipation, seen as a fitting cap to centuries of struggle and hardship. It is, as a result, a natural oversight within the national memory, quietly shed in the postwar years to make room for what

Robert Penn Warren termed the northern "Treasury of Virtue" in Civil War iconography.[11] For Lincoln too, colonization presents a difficult subject, either quietly noted as a remnant of early beliefs that were justly discarded as the war progressed, or pounced upon as a self-evident point of detraction for his racial legacy. With each approach and irrespective of their divergent claims, the haste of reaching a conclusion often overshadows the diligence required to fully assess Lincoln's use of colonization during his presidency, particularly its later years.

Still, Lincoln's colonization endeavors have always been a troublesome part of his legacy, though for different reasons. Early Lincoln biographers generally treated the policy as a matter of fact, noting its existence but also hesitating to pass judgment or even elucidate the reasons for its apparent decline. These topics are conspicuously absent from the biographies by Raymond as well as Nicolay and Hay, though each provide particulars of the projects in Haiti and Panama. Within Lincoln's own generation, the policy became an occasional point of mild detraction for those wishing to differentiate the late president's comparatively moderate views on slavery from the abolitionist wing of the Republican Party. In 1886 George W. Julian, a former congressman and contemporary of the sixteenth president, attempted to qualify Lincoln's antislavery reputation by recounting a link between colonization and the Emancipation Proclamation.[12] In the 1870s Gideon Welles, Lincoln's former secretary of the navy, penned a series of essays for the *Galaxy* magazine in which he defended a tempered view of Lincoln's emancipation policy, colonization included.[13] Welles specifically cautioned against judging Lincoln's moderate approach to emancipation in hindsight. The sheer complexity of the political problems surrounding the abolition of slavery made it fully comprehensible to only those who were present at the time.

Beginning in the middle of the twentieth century many historians began to differentiate between two apparent phases of Lincoln's colonization policy. The first phase encompasses his early political career through the first two years of his presidency, as evidenced by the aforementioned projects in Panama and Haiti as well as frequent references in Lincoln's speeches and writings. The second includes the final two years of Lincoln's life when it is thought that he moved away from colonization, presumably in conjunction with his own personal growth on racial equality. The resultant emphasis of historical inquiry on colonization leans toward the early features of Lincoln's policy such as the 1862 projects.

In great contrast, surprisingly little has been written about Lincoln's colonization policy after January 1, 1863, excepting accounts of the Île à

Vache rescue mission on which the president made no public comment. The resultant void has become a battleground for speculation and controversy. The postemancipation colonization literature remains noticeably underdeveloped, and indeed a topic that many scholars decline to pursue for simple doubt of its existence. To quote the late Philip Shaw Paludan, the "prevailing historical narrative usually ends the story of colonization" with Lincoln's signature on the final Emancipation Proclamation. The signing of this document, which omitted the colonization clause of its precursor of the previous September, has become a symbolic event in its own right as it concerns Lincoln's racial beliefs and a turning point on the particular subject of colonization. So strong is this perception, observed by Paludan, that many leading scholars have aggressively argued against the proposition that Lincoln continued to cling to his earlier colonizationist views in the last two years of his life.[14]

Most historians differ only on the speed with which the proclamation's effects extended to Lincoln's colonization program. Michael Vorenberg has contended that the change was immediate: "In fact, there is no reason to believe that Lincoln ever espoused colonization after he issued the Final Emancipation Proclamation." The case that he did rests upon the "flimsy" evidence of a reputed "colonization interview" in 1865 where Lincoln allegedly spoke to one of his most controversial generals, Benjamin F. Butler, about reviving the project after the Civil War. Other postemancipation evidence usually relies upon speculation about an ambiguous 1864 entry in the diary of John Hay, suggesting Lincoln had moved away from, or, as he put it, "sloughed off" colonization. Vorenberg has argued that this diary date is of little significance even if it comes from a reliable author, as the entry is far removed from any public comment on colonization by the president.[15]

Some historians have identified the proclamation as the starting point of a more gradual evolution in Lincoln's racial views. Eric Foner echoes the consensus on the significance of the January 1, 1863, proclamation, but also suggests that Lincoln "did not immediately abandon the idea." Foner traces Lincoln's pursuit of colonization into the spring of 1863, though after this point he suggests it only consisted of administrative actions on previously existing contracts, such as Île à Vache. As the proclamation's effects became more evident, "Lincoln's commitment to colonization faded in the last two years of the war."[16]

These final two years, beginning with the proclamation or in the early spring of 1863 and ending with Lincoln's assassination in April 1865, are the least understood part of Lincoln's presidency where colonization is concerned. Foner's essay seems to portend an emerging awareness of colonization in the brief months following New Year 1863, though the topic remains lightly researched beyond that and the postemancipation commentary tends to emphasize theories about Lincoln's hypothesized movement away from colonization as a personal belief rather than its fate as a policy. In almost all instances the proclamation is the trigger event for Lincoln's abandonment of the scheme, be it immediate or gradual. As Foner argues, the wake of the proclamation caused Lincoln "to think seriously of the role blacks would play in a postslavery world." His offer of voting rights for black soldiers in 1865 follows naturally, itself a sign that he had taken the prerequisite step of rejecting colonization.[17]

It is still notable that the colonization timeline seems to be expanding, if only slightly. Some historians including Paludan, Mark E. Neely, and Benjamin Quarles have dated Lincoln's last colonization overtures to the early or middle part of 1864.[18] This interpretation derives primarily from the date of Hay's diary entry. Little else is known though about the large gap between the proclamation and the reputed "slough[ing] off." Significantly, Paludan attributes the Hay comment in part to prior setbacks and frustrations in the execution of proposed colonization projects. Still, the overwhelming majority of historians identify the proclamation itself as Lincoln's main turning point.

Two common theories have emerged to explain Lincoln's supposed abandonment of colonization after the final Emancipation Proclamation. The first holds that even prior to the proclamation, Lincoln insincerely advanced colonization "as a device or ploy to make emancipation more palatable to a racist northern electorate," to quote George Fredrickson.[19] According to this "lullaby" argument, Lincoln used the program to signal that the newly emancipated slaves would only reside temporarily among the white population until a new home could be found for them abroad. He never really intended to carry this through, but its suggestion lulled the public's anxiety about emancipation and bought time to prepare them for a more egalitarian racial future.

Though Fredrickson and a handful of other historians ultimately reject this argument, it still occupies a dominant place in Lincoln scholarship. Noted Civil War historian James M. McPherson describes colonization as a "sugar coat" to the proclamation's "strong pill." Gabor Boritt calls it a "lullaby for the antiblack majority," a crafty political palliative to facilitate the "real" goal of emancipation. "Once emancipation was a *fait accompli,* the lullaby had served its purpose."[20]

McPherson has emerged as the most vocal modern proponent of the "lullaby" thesis, lending it his substantial authority among Civil War scholars. To McPherson, even Lincoln's most overt colonizationist statements and actions in 1862 were part of a ruse to "defuse" white backlash. "Lincoln's speech at the White House in August 1862 was intended to soften up the Northern public for an emancipation policy that Lincoln had decided to embrace." Though delivered to a group of black freedmen, it was "really directed" at a "larger white audience" to prepare them for emancipation. Lincoln "did abandon colonization and move partway toward a program of equal rights for freed slaves."[21]

A second popular explanation holds that Lincoln abandoned colonization after undergoing a change of heart on race. This thesis concedes that Lincoln originally believed that the white and black races "should be separated" to the betterment of both, as he told a "Deputation of Negroes" at the White House in August 1862.[22] The frustrating results of the Île à Vache and Chiriquí contracts undoubtedly dampened his enthusiasm for colonization toward the end of his presidency, but he is also asserted to have undergone a moral reckoning in the Emancipation Proclamation's wake and accepted the United States' multiracial future. "[T]he change," notes Fredrickson, "may also have reflected a transformation of Lincoln's basic attitude toward blacks and his conception of their future in American society." Both Foner and Fredrickson contend that the performance of black soldiers on the battlefield deeply moved Lincoln. He abandoned colonization of blacks because of its fundamental inconsistency with asking the very same population to fight for their country. "Although he made no public admission of his change of heart," continues Fredrickson, "Lincoln, it appears, was one of the converts."[23]

Both theories attach finality to Lincoln's colonization programs after the Emancipation Proclamation, be it immediate or as an inescapable evolution in his policy. As a result, Lincoln remains personally absent from the colonization story after January 1863, excepting the rescue of the Île à Vache survivors. Recent scholarship has returned to the controversial topic of General Benjamin F. Butler's claimed "colonization interview," exposing the possibility that Lincoln's interest revived in April 1865 a few days before his assassination. Butler remains a troublesome source for most historians though, his reminiscence plagued by a penchant for exaggeration and its sheer distance in time from the actual event.[24] Otherwise, the colonization narrative from 1863 to 1865 is largely nonexistent. The possibility of additional colonization projects, undertaken at Lincoln's instigation after the Chiriquí and Île à

Vache contracts of 1862, is all but entirely precluded by the two prevailing theses and the usually reliable testimony of Hay and Nicolay.

This text tells the story of one such unnoticed project, initiated in early 1863 at the exact moment Lincoln is widely believed to have begun a move away from colonization. Just three weeks after signing the Emancipation Proclamation, Lincoln personally approached the British minister to the United States to discuss a joint venture between the two nations in the Caribbean. Lincoln knew that the agricultural colonies of the British West Indies were perpetually plagued by labor shortages and offered a proposition. The two countries would reach an agreement to resettle the slaves freed by the proclamation by encouraging and subsidizing their voluntary migration to the colony of British Honduras. In return for this labor, crown-backed land companies would supply the freedmen with parcels to be earned over time from their agricultural produce. Of equal importance, Lincoln evidently believed that the British colonies would provide stronger protections for the rights of the freedmen than would the postwar South.

This little-known West Indies "emigration" project signified an evolution in Lincoln's colonization policies, though not as most historians have supposed. It portended a new approach to the same policy, taking into account lessons learned in the previous several months. British Honduras was but the first and most advanced example in a "second wave" of proposed colonies, wherein the United States would enter into partnership with foreign governments to encourage the emigration of free blacks to designated sites in the Caribbean. The colony of British Guiana soon joined the negotiations. Not long after, Lincoln directed the State Department to present a proposal with similar features to the Netherlands for their neighboring South American colony of Surinam.[25]

Work on these projects progressed over the next year, often aided by the president's direct encouragement and approval. In the summer of 1863 there was even talk in Washington of presenting a colonization treaty with the Dutch government to the Senate for ratification. By January 1864, agents in British Honduras and Guiana spoke openly of the impending arrival of the first ships of emancipated slaves, and a team of recruiters stood ready in three northern port cities to facilitate their transport with the assistance of the U.S. Emigration Office.

One need not possess familiarity with these forgotten projects to know that they passed into history without achieving their purpose. This lost round of colonization unraveled well into the second half of Lincoln's presidency, just as the chosen settlements sat on the verge of receiving their first freedmen laborers. Curiously, the instigating causes of their eventual abandonment had little to do with an Emancipation Proclamation-induced change of heart in Lincoln's thinking, or the exhaustion of the "lullaby's" political purpose. Rather, the West Indies strategy died amidst bitter political infighting between Lincoln's subordinates within the bureaucracy of the Interior Department, and a related decision of Congress to repeal the colonization budget.

Given the exhaustive historical scrutiny that Abraham Lincoln's presidency has received, the 1863–1864 Caribbean colonization projects are an unlikely oversight. Yet for reasons of historical accident and a diffuse volume of primary records, neglect has befallen this final wave of the U.S. government's actual colonization policies. Historians have long known that Lincoln considered British Honduras, Guiana, Surinam, and several other West Indies locations as prospective emigration points for freed slaves in 1862, though most mistake a lack of accessible documentation for proof of their early rejection. They are accordingly grouped among the "other" paths not taken in colonization lore. Nicolay and Hay include them among a lengthy list of "various propositions . . . to the Department of State offering lands for such colonization," none of which presumably materialized. Most historians since then have followed the presidential secretaries' lead by acknowledging the discussion of proposals from multiple Caribbean colonies but asserting that they died in their infancy for a variety of different, and usually mistaken, political reasons.[26]

The British Honduras settlement was by far the most developed of the Caribbean colonization schemes at the time of its collapse, and left a sufficiently accessible documentary record that a handful of historians have happened upon the early stages of its proposal. Unfortunately, its paper trail is a perilous one where it is common to mistake a dry lead for the premature demise of the project itself. Thus, where acknowledged at all, the British Honduras project is thought not to have advanced beyond a preliminary exchange of letters between colonial agents and the U.S. government at the project's outset. Its failure is usually attributed to either Lincoln or a cabinet secretary eventually turning the project away in early 1863 after recognizing the demand for black soldiers in the Union army, though the evidence for this conclusion has been, in each case, mistaken.[27] Excepting this scant literature on British Honduras, Lincoln's colonization projects in the West Indies remain an entirely new discovery for Civil War scholarship. Practically nothing at all has been written of the less developed proposals in Guiana and Surinam.[28]

The forgotten story of Lincoln's last major colonization push provides a bridge across what has thus far been a gaping void in the study of colonization, as well as a perennial source of controversy among historians: the status of Lincoln's policy in the critical period between the Emancipation Proclamation and his death in 1865. The Caribbean projects bear note for their significance in relation to better-known predecessors, as they continued to attract political interest after the Île à Vache colony was deemed a failure. Furthermore, the British Honduras settlement actually came closer to fruition than did any aspect of the more-famous Chiriquí contract.

With equal significance, the story of Caribbean colonization provides an occasion for the study of Lincoln's personal beliefs on race and slavery and the troublesome question of their final disposition at his death. It is also a story of administrative and diplomatic politics, telling how governments and interests spanning three continents resolved their respective stakes in colonization, and thus determined its influence on the racial and economic futures of each.

Chapter 2

American Freedmen, British Labor

In the summer of 1862 Abraham Lincoln approached James Mitchell, his newly appointed commissioner of emigration, with the task of administering the recently appropriated colonization fund.[1] The two men were old acquaintances from a prior era of midwestern colonization politics, set to embark on the second decade of their professional relationship. Mitchell was the scion of a feisty Protestant family from Londonderry, Ireland. He immigrated to the United States by way of Philadelphia in 1837, took up the cloth of the Methodist Episcopal church, and became an antislavery preacher in Indiana, advocating "gradual emancipation and colonization" in the mold of Henry Clay. An 1848 foray into the political realm landed him a position as secretary of the American Colonization Society for Indiana, where he shepherded a procolonization referendum into the state's constitution in 1852.[2]

Lincoln's emigration agent was something of a paradox, astute as he was stubborn and prone to both brilliance and obstinacy. A consummate colonizationist driven by a genuine conviction that he was working for the betterment of African Americans, he was also a curiosity in a movement sometimes known for its inseparable blending of economic motives into its claimed moral calling. An antislavery Democrat, a racial separatist who befriended and employed African Americans, and a clergyman immersed in a world of business contracts and diplomacy, Mitchell charted an unlikely career before ending not far from his origin, a small rural church differing only by state. He was a British-educated gentleman in a world apart, riding the Methodist circuit on the American frontier for most of his life. He spent almost three decades in the company of the leading politicians and statesmen of the day, both infuriating his adversaries and endearing himself to the political allies that he had a knack for finding. It is not difficult to see why Lincoln hit it off with a man possessing such an unusual combination of quirk and fervor. Illinois' favorite son often preferred the rougher edges of frontier politicking to the procedural stuffiness and decorum of Washington, and Mitchell certainly had little patience for procedure.

The two first crossed paths in July 1853 when Mitchell visited Springfield, seeking to expand his colonization work further west. When he inquired for assistance to "aid me in my work in Illinois as Joseph A. Wright had aided me in his State," a local minister directed him to "an attorney named Abraham Lincoln." As Mitchell recounted:

> We proceeded to the public square of the town and as we leisurely walked forward along its best-built side Mr. Dodge pointed out a gentleman seated on a dry goods box five or six doors ahead of us, saying as he did so: "There sits Mr. Lincoln." My friend had previously eulogized the attorney very highly, yet when I saw his great, gaunt and angular figure, loosely if not carelessly dressed, I was not favorably impressed and said to myself: 'If that is Illinois' great man, Illinois is not much.'[3]

A subsequent introduction quickly shattered Mitchell's preconception though, and upon finding their views in agreement the two men parted as friends. The following Sunday Rev. Mitchell gave a brief colonization sermon at Springfield's First Presbyterian Church, which the Lincoln family sometimes attended. Upon the talk's conclusion Lincoln handed Mitchell a three-dollar contribution to purchase an ACS membership for the church's pastor, Rev. James A. Smith.[4]

They remained in contact until Lincoln's election to the presidency, and in 1861 Lincoln recommended Mitchell for a political appointment. "James Mitchell," he informed William Seward, "I know and like. He was, for years, colonization agent, for Indiana."[5] Mitchell's original appointment documents have been lost, but he joined the Lincoln administration before Congress officially sanctioned colonization, perhaps as early as December 1861. On August 4, 1862, Mitchell received what he described as an "amended commission" from the president to administer the newly created colonization fund.[6]

The subject of entering into a colonization partnership with Great Britain was first presented to Lincoln by Mitchell in July 1862. The minister broached the idea of soliciting support from British Caribbean colonies, as he regarded Britain to be the "next best friend of the negro race." He ascribed a strong endorsement to the president, who was reported to have exclaimed, "If England wants our negroes, and will do better by them than we can, I say let her have them, and may God bless her."[7] The reliability of this utterance carries with it the caution due to any recollected quotation of the late president, though it evinces a sentiment that both the British and American governments eventually acted upon.

Unbeknownst to Mitchell, the British Colonial Office was already taking an interest in recruiting freedmen laborers from the United States. The British West Indian empire of free-labor plantations suffered a constant shortage of manpower and held out hope of obtaining a supply of agriculturally proficient black workers from the soon-to-be emancipated population in sections of the southern United States. That same month Edward John Eyre, the lieutenant governor of Jamaica, approached the Duke of Newcastle, secretary of state for the colonies, with a plan to provide "passage-money" for the transportation of black immigrants from the United States. Cognizant of existing colonization proposals in Haiti and the Dutch Caribbean holdings, Eyre suggested that the "stream of emigration . . . might be diverted to Jamaica and other West Indian Islands requiring population."[8] Eyre's scheme initially elicited the support of planters in Jamaica itself, though London envisioned a broader emigration policy involving its Caribbean holdings as determined by their needs for labor. Subsequent iterations of the scheme devolved upon colonial authorities in Jamaica, British Honduras, and British Guiana, each tailoring their proposals to their respective colonies. In London Newcastle and Earl Russell, the foreign secretary, stood watch for a signal on the Lincoln administration's position from Lord Lyons, the British minister at Washington. It would become a game of patience for Britain, taking care not to press the issue prematurely and ever doubting that they would receive a "clearer view" of support from an American government that seemed preoccupied with the pending Chiriquí contract.[9]

For American Secretary of State William Seward, rumors about the approaching British offer appeared as yet another colonization venture on a crowded plate that already included proposals in Chiriquí, Haiti, Dutch Surinam, Liberia, and Ecuador, among others. Britain presented the advantages of a common language and an established English law colonial system, perceived by those in Washington to provide sufficient securities for the rights of black colonists. Though careful to avoid any commitment, Seward informed the British Legation on September 4 that "if emigration did take place, the British Colonies would be more likely to suit [the freedmen] . . . than any other colonies."[10]

The secretary of state personally expressed his reservations about the project, much as he did with all colonization matters. Seward was no colonizationist. He would later describe his policy relationship with Lincoln by noting, "Once only did we disagree in sentiment . . . His 'colonization' scheme."[11] The secretary similarly informed William Stuart, the legation's *chargé d'affaires*, that he privately doubted the feasibility of colonization "although he knew that the President and other members of the Cabinet would not agree with him." He nonetheless agreed to carry out the president's wishes and informed the British government that any offer to receive colonists would "meet with proper attention," and possibly precedence. Stuart accordingly advised Russell to offer an indication that "Her Majesty's Government will at any time be ready to co-operate in carrying out the President's benevolent schemes by consenting to receive a portion of the negroes upon terms to be hereafter agreed upon."[12]

A week's passage provided an opportunity for Stuart to confer with Kansas Senator Samuel Pomeroy, himself serving an unusual dual role as a colonization agent for the Chiriquí contract, and again broach the subject with Seward. The secretary of state reported that he recently found Lincoln "still anxious to carry out" the then-pending Chiriquí project, though he correctly anticipated its troubles amidst growing opposition from neighboring Central American governments. Should these fears be realized, the British colonies would become an appealing alternative. With Lincoln warming to the British proposals, Seward informed Stuart: "[I]t would be sufficient in effect that agents, with proper authority from Her Majesty's Government, should come here, and endeavor, with the permission of the Federal Government, to organize Colonies by inviting free negroes to emigrate in the same manner as had been done by Senator Pomeroy."[13]

On September 22 the president asked his cabinet's views on colonization, and the Caribbean proposals of the Dutch and British governments in particular. Lincoln rebuffed the suggestion of Edward Bates, the attorney general, to make colonization a program of compulsory deportation. Instead, he endorsed a policy of "emigration" which "must be voluntary and without expense" to the applicants. Lincoln initially favored establishing a formal treaty with individual European powers, though this introduced the political uncertainty of Senate ratification. Gideon Welles, secretary of the navy, suggested that the program's voluntary nature required only the consent of the "emigrant who chose to leave our shores" and could be conducted under a simple contract or agreement without need for congressional action.[14]

Per Lincoln's request, Bates prepared a memorandum on the government's legal options and submitted it to Seward at the next cabinet meeting.

A narrowly tailored treaty carried the benefit of stronger legal assurances for the emigrants and to the U.S. government. It obliged other signatories to the policy's terms and solidified the "channels of trade and friendly intercourse" with the foreign power, a much-touted secondary motive for colonization. No existing laws prohibited simple emigration though, and many foreign powers might simply accept black laborers on those terms.[15]

On September 27 Seward again approached the legation to announce that the United States would soon be "ready to conclude a Convention with Great Britain" providing for assurances of the "freedom of the negroes, their protection and kind treatment, and their location on healthy soil."[16] Constrained to the delicate phraseology of diplomacy, the British Legation restated the American line wherein colonization became an act of "compassion" to a troubled and enslaved "African race."

For Britain, the path to obtaining its desired labor force was strewn with political hazard and pitfall. By all indication, Lincoln desired to colonize the "contrabands"—former slaves who attained their freedom by falling behind or escaping to the Union lines with the controversial legal status of being "seized property." These laborers were also considered the most appealing, as they knew the trades of agriculture from slavery and, in many cases, had cultivated the same crops—sugar, cotton, and rice. Though the Colonial Office recognized this as a benefit, the Foreign Office knew that their freedom came at great cost to the southern Confederacy by design and, thus, presented a source of "embarrassing complications" for a foreign power wishing to maintain its diplomatic distance from the raging Civil War. All pretense of "benevolence" aside, Stuart privately confided to Russell that any agreement would serve the coinciding purpose of drawing Britain into "a common act of hostility" with the United States government against the South.[17]

While the labor of the rebel states was desired, it remained out of reach barring drastic changes in the legal status of the slaves and the tide of the war itself. Antislavery campaigners in England took notice of the proposed policy's implications as well and lambasted the foreign secretary's apparent deference to the Confederacy:

> It must be the Confederates of whom our Government stands in fear. The emigrants could be their property alone—and they only would have any interest in, or any pretence to the reclamation of the fugitives. So that it is really, as we have said, a practical question whether or not England shall acknowledge the right of one human

> being to hold property in another. We are deeply ashamed to have to ask whether such a motive shall be allowed to continue, to influence the action of this country, or of its colonies. It is certain—a shameful certainty—that for the moment it does prevail over every consideration of interest, of humanity, and of honor.[18]

Russell justified his hesitation with political pragmatism. The war's outcome was far from certain at this point, and Britain had to anticipate the possibility of a future in which the Confederacy established its independence. Still, the fortunes of the battlefield dictated only half of the labor scenario; future colonization appeared to be intertwined with the execution of the proposed Emancipation Proclamation—a view shared by many on the American side of the negotiating table including, possibly, Lincoln himself.[19]

Seward's long-anticipated offer arrived on September 30 in a widely disseminated circular to Charles Francis Adams, U.S minister at the Court of St. James' in London. This document contained the legal stipulations for all subsequent agreements. The State Department would initiate negotiations to establish a system of recruitment for free black laborers wishing to relocate to designated tropical colonies in the Caribbean. Colonization was to take place on a voluntary basis under the direction of British agents "appointed by this Government or with its sanction." In return for receiving permission, recruiters would be required to provide proper transportation and dwelling spaces for the freedmen emigrants, along with assurances to protect their individual rights and liberties. The Chiriquí contract's immediacy still assured its priority in Lincoln's mind, but Seward's circular laid the foundations for a long-term migration program, perhaps lasting ten years or more under the terms he authorized Adams to present to Russell.[20]

London responded to the circular with deliberate caution, having received word from the legation in Washington that "it appears improbable that any negroes will be induced to emigrate from America" barring the further change in its two impediments, the war and the status of American emancipation policies.[21] Seward's circular nonetheless provided a sufficient first step, and while it theoretically encompassed all British holdings in the tropics as well as those of other European powers, two British colonies eagerly acted upon it in anticipation of an impending agreement.

The colonial economy of British Honduras was inextricably linked to the production of mahogany. At midcentury this staple, along with logwood, accounted for over 80 percent of the colony's exports until it became mired in a continuous state of depression following the deforestation of the 1840s and '50s and the end of the British "Railway Mania," which had driven demand for mahogany carriages. In 1859 a merchant and landowner named John Hodge registered the British Honduras Company (BHC) and hired a conveyancer to revise the land statutes of the colony with the intent of changing its fortunes and capitalizing on the result. The Honduras Land Title Acts of 1858–1861 enabled the BHC to rapidly consolidate the colony's lands, with the intent of converting them to sugar and cotton production.[22]

Hodge was apparently something of a controversial figure in British Honduras. In 1849 he entered into the partnership of Hyde, Hodge and Company, which had been instrumental in instigating the recruitment of labor for the West Indies in Africa, and which signed an agreement with the British government to place recaptives from the international slave trade in Caribbean apprenticeships. This represented the culmination of a move away from older British policy of settling such people in Sierra Leone but was a predictable result of the ongoing and extreme West Indian manpower shortage. This contract with a single company, which would actually end up being the Colonial Office's solution to the hitherto chronic question of how to manage liberated Africans, marked an attempt on its part to avoid the inconsistent quality of private emigration vessels. But, as with others, it also gave Hyde, Hodge and Company a vested interest in pushing the limits of acceptable and noncoercive recruitment, and in a foreseeable irony, a British government report of 1854 had to record accusations of slave-trading against the company. In any case, that trade was in decline by the mid-1850s—the emigration system with it, naturally—and private ventures once again muscled in on the business.[23] Hodge's Belizean concerns were in fact one of the victims of the colony's depression of that era, failing in 1856 and thus engendering "the ill will and distrust of two-thirds of this community" toward him for some years to come; his resurrection as manager of the BHC was one backed by metropolitan capital and the new speculation-friendly laws that he helped to introduce.[24]

During this period Hodge proved a headache for the government of British Honduras—granted official colonial status in 1862—petitioning the Privy Council in London for repayment of crown license fees for mahogany logging on lands that he later claimed to have already owned and going down the same route in a separate attempt to claim nine years of back pay as the agent of the settlement in Britain from 1848 to 1857.[25] Nevertheless, given the increasingly monopolistic power of the

BHC in the colony, his influence and that of the company were great indeed.

By the early 1860s the free labor plantations of Hodge's business plan were well known to speculators. In 1862 a New York trader named Aaron Columbus Burr approached Lincoln with a plan to colonize freed slaves on a tract he purchased in the colony. The contract, offered to the Interior Department for $75,000 and incessantly promoted by the effusive pamphleteering of Washington socialite Anna Ella Carroll, attracted the attention of Mitchell in his office's annual report for 1862 but was soon eclipsed as the administration focused its energies on Chiriquí.[26]

The BHC took notice of the Burr proposal though, and anticipating Washington's growing interest in colonization, they began to prepare an offer of their own with the advantageous sanction of Her Majesty's Government. Prodded by Hodge, the colonial legislature adopted an Immigration Act on September 5 for the purpose of encouraging the "immigration of agricultural and other laborers into the colony of British Honduras at the expense of private persons." The law authorized Frederick Seymour, the colony's lieutenant governor, to proclaim foreign ports of emigration where authorized agents of companies such as the BHC could recruit and transfer emigrant laborers.[27] Though technically open-ended, the Immigration Act was plainly intended to apply to ports within the United States. Seymour indicated as much on October 15 when he requested permission from the Colonial Office "to introduce coloured labourers under this act from the United States." "Why we should go to the other end of the world to procure the labour we require . . . I can hardly say," he continued in a subsequent letter; "President Lincoln wishes to deport a large number of coloured persons from the United States to Central America."[28]

Colonial authorities in British Guiana approached the prospect of receiving colonists with similar enthusiasm. Unlike Honduras, Guiana's extensive sugar plantation system dated to the colony's founding by the Dutch in the seventeenth century. Britain emancipated the colony's large slave system in 1834 and converted its economy to a nominally free-labor sugar production. Thereafter the planter class used indenture laws and a strict regulatory regime to effectively preserve the old plantation model, prompting novelist Anthony Trollope's 1859 assessment of the colony as a "mild despotism, tempered by sugar."[29]

After 1834 the colony's large sugar enterprise outpaced the existing population of ex-slaves, creating a constant demand for laborers and causing authorities to seek their importation from India, China, and other holdings of the British Empire. The colony accordingly welcomed reports of Lincoln's interest in colonization and with strong encouragement from T. D. Edwards, the U.S. consul in Demerara, submitted a proposal of its own. The Guiana plan elicited the cautious optimism of Sir Francis Hincks, the colony's governor. After a meeting with Edwards at the consulate, Hincks commissioned Colonial Secretary William Walker to travel to Washington and inquire about the prospects of an immigration agreement. Unlike Honduras, which was introducing crops to old mahogany lands, Guiana already commanded a sizable agricultural operation. Edwards commended the colony to Washington as favorably suited for liberated slaves of the south's sugar-producing regions. "The negro could command more than twice as much as either Coolie or Chinese," he informed Seward, in reference to Britain's other prospective labor sources.[30]

Walker arrived in Washington to much disappointment, discovering that "reports, which had reached British Guyana with regard to the number of Negroes available for emigration, had been greatly exaggerated." He appeared at the British Legation a day before Seward's circular and at a time when Stuart remained skeptical as to whether an agreement would ever materialize.[31] Walker nonetheless presented his colony's proposal to Caleb Blood Smith, the secretary of the interior, and to Mitchell. Smith considered the offer premature but remarked that the administration had a "disposition favourably to entertain the matter." His lone stipulation was that the Americans reach a "convention" with Britain rather than dealing with individual territorial proposals on a case-by-case basis.[32]

Though Walker departed without his desired agreement, he also took Smith's words as a sign of growing interest. He appointed Samuel R. Dickson, a New York merchant who did business in Guiana, "to take over the work" should "an opening for emigration . . . present itself" in his absence. The secretary maintained contact with Mitchell through the spring and directed Dickson to work with the Emigration Office. His reports to London also prompted Newcastle to place all colonial agents under the direction of the Foreign Office by way of the British Legation in Washington to prepare for Lincoln's desired convention.[33]

The Colonial Office's early enthusiasm hit a brick wall under Russell's charge. Fearful that an agreement would disrupt Britain's attempt to peaceably straddle the raging Civil War, the foreign secretary held out for a clearer sign that the terms of any agreement would favor Britain or at least spare it from imposition. Pressing the matter "would at present be inexpedient," and could draw Britain into the politically treacherous "contrabands" issue. "We must not expose ourselves to any charge of kidnapping," he wrote Stuart, insisting that colonists "must be men already free in the U.S." Russell apparently underestimated the significance of the September 30 circular at the time and rebuffed an attempt by Charles Francis Adams to enter into the proposed "convention" on October 30.[34] A cold reception to the initial presentation of the document caused Adams to respond to Seward that he considered "his lordship's answer as definitively closing the matter."[35] When the text of Seward's offer finally reached Russell a week later, the foreign secretary cautiously reexamined the American offer, tepidly directing Lyons to receive all colonial representatives in consultation as he awaited clearer signals from Lincoln.

By November panicked farmers in British Honduras clamored for labor, lest their lands sit idle through another growing season. Hodge pled their case with the Colonial Office, writing "we most earnestly beg that you will move" Russell. "[O]ur hopes of planting the cotton-seed sent, and cutting the sugar cane now growing, are centred in obtaining the labourers we can procure in the United States." The Duke of Newcastle's secretary "lost no time" in communicating this request to Russell and directed him to inform the BHC manager of the difficulties anticipated by the Foreign Office. "It is possible that the commencement might be expedited by your proceeding at once to Washington," he continued, "and placing yourself in communication with Lord Lyons." Hodge acted on the suggestion in late November and prepared to depart "in order to test the possibility of obtaining labourers." He would seek Lyons's direction "before bringing the Act of the Honduras Legislature into operation," per the requirements of the Foreign Office.[36]

Hodge does not appear to have filed the specifics of the BHC plan with London, and perhaps this comes as no surprise, since not only was he trying to seize a novel opportunity as quickly as possible, but he may have been aware too of the heavy tweaking that it would require once he was in America. The closest sense of his rationale as explained to the Colonial Office comes in an annotation by one of its secretaries, Sir Frederic Rogers, written on the back of a letter: "He seems to know the southern and northern states and to have access to their principal (abolitionist) politicians. He declares that they will persevere in the emancipation policy. That Missouri adopts that policy and that the blacks are leaving that state—and (passing of south Illinois) are making their way eastward. That the same process is going on in Kentucky and part of Tennessee . . . and that "the stampede" as he expresses of negroes from the provinces further south may be expected a few months later." Rogers added that he had thought this worth writing down as an example of how an enterprising man seemed willing to risk his own money and that of others on a potentially imprudent scheme and was aware of his previous business failure. Not for the last time, a British government official expressed very real doubts as to his prospects, yet such concerns were generally qualified by the hope that they might be proven wrong.[37]

Unenthused by the apparent lack of direction from Lincoln, Lyons remained duly skeptical of ever obtaining an agreement for the Colonial Office, now referred to as "Newcastle's plan." Seward informed him of lingering divisions in the cabinet on December 26 and suggested that a clear policy was unlikely until after Congress adjourned on March 4. When informed of the Immigration Act from British Honduras, Seward "answered that he supposed there would be no objection to allowing private persons" to recruit black laborers but could not at this time agree to a formal policy. At Seward's suggestion, Lyons drafted a general statement on the "views of Her Majesty's Government" regarding emigration with the intent that they be presented at a politically ripe moment. Though quick to deprecate the "extremely doubtful" prospects of colonization in the face of a growing demand for black laborers at home and an anticipated policy of employing them on the field as soldiers, the secretary of state offered a frank political assessment of Lincoln's intentions. "Many . . . might, and indeed the President himself, be inclined to the opinion that the most desirable thing for both the races was to separate them, and to reserve North America exclusively for the whites."[38]

As Hodge set to embark, the Colonial Office informed him that the prospects were "not encouraging" by way of Lyons's latest dispatch. He nonetheless obtained assurances that the Foreign Office would sanction the recruitment of contrabands, provided that the emigration canvassers adhere to some geographical limitations. Should he succeed in swaying the U.S. government, the cities of New York, Boston, and Philadelphia could be proclaimed "as ports from which emigration may proceed." Politics precluded recruitment south of Philadelphia and kept the desirable labor supply of the plantation South out of reach, even in places the Union controlled such as New Orleans. Even with this concession Hodge still needed full cooperation from Washington lest he simply repeat Walker's mission and depart without labor. For the time being, American inaction and British timidity had slowed the policy into a state of stagnation.[39]

Chapter 3

Mr. Lincoln's Hobby

Upon receiving word of the January 1, 1863, Emancipation Proclamation, Lord Lyons wryly remarked that it "frees the slaves in all the states or parts of the states in which the United States government has at the present moment no *de facto* power." The legation recognized its significance only as a political gamble and speculated about its feared effect of sparking a violent backlash among northern whites.[1] The new policy's much-speculated relation to colonization received no mention in the reports back to London. "Newcastle's plan" appeared to linger in indeterminacy as it had for many months prior until the highest American authority lent it his considerable weight.

Though long characterized as a "transformative" event for Lincoln's views, the Emancipation Proclamation had little immediate effect on the administration's colonization policy. Lincoln identified the goals of that policy in his annual address to Congress on December 1, 1862. He alluded to the collapse of the Chiriquí project with disappointment, noting that "several of the Spanish American Republics have protested against the sending of such colonies to their respective territories." Colonization still remained his administration's policy, though its focus would shift to Haiti, Liberia, and an emerging "emigration" project in the Caribbean. Lincoln made no reference to Britain by name, but his remarks clearly alluded to what the British Legation knew as "Newcastle's plan." "I have at the same time offered to the several States situated within the Tropics, or having colonies there, to negotiate with them, subject to the advice and consent of the Senate, to favor the voluntary emigration of persons of that class to their respective territories, upon conditions which shall be equal, just, and humane."[2] Lincoln said little more in public about the British negotiations, or any colonization scheme for that matter. This silence and the absence of any colonization clauses in the final Emancipation Proclamation have been mistakenly interpreted as the first sign of Lincoln's changing views. Yet the events of January 1863 offer no indication of any new policies save for those Lincoln presented to Congress a month prior.

The Interior Department approached colonization as if it were business as usual after the proclamation, albeit under a new head. Caleb Smith resigned the post due to poor health effective December 31. Lincoln elevated Smith's assistant John Palmer Usher with little fanfare, as Usher too hailed from Indiana, ensuring its continued representation in the cabinet. Furthermore, the new secretary effectively took on many of Smith's tasks in late 1862 as a result of his illness. Usher had the appearance and excitement of a quintessential bureaucrat according to Noah Brooks, a journalist who befriended Lincoln in 1862 and gained an inside vantage of his administration. He was "fair, fat, fifty and florid, well fed, unctuous, a good worker, as good a liver, an able lawyer, an accidental member of the Cabinet by the law of succession, and is socially dignified and reservedly get-at-able."[3] The new secretary busied himself with the administrative duties of his office and generally stayed clear of public political battles, though like Smith he believed in colonization. He spent the first months of 1863 finalizing the Île à Vache contract that Smith had initiated the previous year.[4] Unbeknownst to him, Lincoln already had a new colonization priority.

"The President told me the other day that he wanted to have an informal talk with me," read a confidential January 23 letter from Lyons to London. The official dispatches steered clear of this development, and nothing about the meeting's purpose was explicitly conveyed by Lincoln, though the British minister had a reason to deduce one. The invitation arrived with a copy of James Mitchell's 1862 report on colonization, outlining pending proposals, including those in British Honduras and Guiana. "The subject of the talk will no doubt be his hobby," quipped Lyons, "the exportation of the Contrabands."[5]

This presidential invitation offered Lyons the first clear indicator in months that the Americans intended for the proposed "convention" to proceed. "I think something may be done on the Duke of Newcastle's Plan," he continued, so long as the appointed agents remained under British supervision and did not attempt to draw laborers from the Confederacy directly. "It is from the Southern ports, that the President most wishes to send Negroes." To proclaim New Orleans as a port of departure, however, would endanger England's position of distance from the war itself. Therefore Lyons decided to "throw cold water upon this scheme" until he received further directions from London and specifics from the president.[6]

On January 26 Lincoln sent word to Mitchell that he required unspecified papers from the Emigration Office "in advance of a meeting he proposes to have with Lord Lyons today."[7] Mindful of the delicate diplomacy involved,

Lincoln prepared to offer the scheme in an open "informal" discussion to solicit the British government's position. Lyons exhaustively detailed the president's views in his next dispatch to London:

> The President of the United States sent for me yesterday, and upon my presenting myself, told me that he had been for some time anxious to speak to me in an informal and unofficial manner on the subject of promoting the emigration of colored people from this country to British colonies. He would begin he said by observing that he could very well understand that Great Britain objected, under present circumstances, to engage to receive Negroes who were claimed by Southern owners as slaves. Were he in our position, he should feel the same objection; but he would ask me whether we were really desirous to receive other people of colour; people who had either been born free or had become so with the consent of their former owners . . .
>
> . . . The President proceeded to say that this [desire] being the case, he would ask whether we were prepared to enter into arrangements with the Government of the United States, provided we could avoid all at risk of the complications which might be caused if we received Africans claimed as slaves.[8]

Lincoln had made the anticipated offer, and Britain was ready to move on the plan but not as previously discussed. Lyons saw little necessity for a "formal convention" between the two governments, favoring only an agreement of terms before commencing emigration. He knew, as did Lincoln, that the convention would require the Senate's ratification. The Confederacy's reaction provided greater cause for concern though, and though he avoided mention of this complication to Lincoln, Lyons knew the Foreign Office would have no part in a treaty that publicly obliged Her Majesty's Government to the North's emancipation policies. He could appeal to the Americans' desire for rapid results though. Why pursue the needless complications of a convention when a simple agreement under the existing laws could attain the same results? "All that seemed requisite," he continued, "was that the United States Government, on their side, should establish such rules for the guidance of their own emigration office, as should be sufficient to guard the Negroes from being imposed upon by unauthorized agents, and that Her Majesty's Government, on the other side, should authorize the colonial governments to send suitable agents here."

These agents would act under the direction of suitable authorities in the United States, likely Mitchell's Emigration Office. British colonial funds would be used to transport the colonists in exchange for a contractual period of work. Lincoln agreed with Lyons's concern that free blacks would require further incentives to transplant in number, but "the only way to ascertain," he told the British minister, "would be to try the experiment." The task of carrying the policy through devolved upon Seward and Usher. With the scheme ripe to commence, Lyons immediately proceeded to the State Department to lay down "what had passed" in his conversation with Lincoln.[9]

Despite the interview's informal nature, it convinced London of Lincoln's personal attention to the negotiations and his continued commitment to colonization. Nor was this commitment isolated, as the president continued to investigate other channels for the policy. On January 30 Lincoln met with Thomas Malcom of the Pennsylvania Colonization Society. Their brief interview concerned a proposed "colony on the St. John's river in Liberia." Lincoln granted him two hundred dollars for the Rev. Chancey Leonard, the African American pastor of Washington's First Baptist Church, to investigate the site.[10]

A week passed before Lyons approached Usher about his interview with the president. Somewhat startled, he found the secretary of the interior completely unprepared for their ensuing discussion. The British minister had witnessed the first of many instances where Seward, or perhaps even Lincoln himself, failed to communicate further directions on the project to a subordinate tasked with its administration. Lyons begrudgingly explained the British proposition, although with Usher's welcome. The secretary "appeared to be disposed to further removal of the coloured race." Both men acknowledged the difficulty of increasing migration's appeal among the free black population. Perhaps the two governments could entice "intelligent and influential" black leaders to visit Honduras and Guiana, offering them and "their countrymen" the prospects of political freedom and an "improvement in their social position."[11]

In mid-February Seward belatedly brought Usher into agreement that the project should wait until Congress's adjournment on March 4 and "begged" Lyons, none too eager in his own right save for the Colonial Office's pressures, not to press forward until then.[12] The legation waited anyway for Hodge's anticipated arrival in April and bided their time with administrative preparations. In response to Seward's request, the Foreign Office provided a general memorandum on the British government's position. London would agree "that private persons should be permitted by the Government of the United States to obtain in those States colored emigrants and to enter into contracts with such emigrants for service for three years in the British West

Indian Colonies; the emigration being placed under the control of Her Majesty's Legation at Washington and under such superintendence by paid agents—appointed by each or all of the Colonies, as may be sufficient to prevent abuse."[13]

By every indication the Americans welcomed the proposed terms. Usher committed his department, informing Seward that "I regard the proposition with favor."[14] As March 4 passed, Seward notified the legation of the Interior Department's intent to "cooperate cordially in carrying out" this arrangement and asked Lyons to contemplate his government's obligations to protect the rights of any colonists they received. Usher responded approvingly when presented with a copy of the British Honduras Immigration Act and a summary of existing laws in British Guiana, hesitating only to note that his government's cautious pace was a necessity due to the profusion of "speculators who, while pretending to be friends of the Negro, in reality sought" federal colonization funds for "their own interest." [15] The British West Indies project, diligently planned under the eye and sanction of both governments, would guard against this recurrence.

The wait until March 4 proved to be a restless one for planters in British Honduras. Charles Leas, the U.S. consul in Belize City, informed the State Department of a "great anxiety" among the local population over the rumored policies of the president. From Seward's vantage, Leas provided justification for the lethargic pace of the current negotiations. "If the Government of the United States is to lend her countenance to the deportation, or emigration, of the colored population," warned the consul, "it should be carefully seen to that there is a tangible prospect . . . of their condition being bettered." Leas feared that the laborers could easily become vulnerable to low wages and neglect, a situation he believed to be emerging in Jamaica. He nonetheless saw the colony as a strong candidate for colonization, describing it as "the country for the black man" so long as the two governments established safeguards for the emigrants' welfare.[16]

In London, the Foreign Office's Russell and U.S. Minister Adams supplied Hodge with introductory letters to their respective officers in Washington.[17] Two BHC agents in Belize City similarly sought approval from Consul Leas, who submitted an attestation of Hodge's character to Washington at their request and outlined the project as it had been described to him. From this early stage forward, Leas assumed the duty of ensuring the protection of the colonists as American citizens. Any labor contract, he insisted, must contain provisions for transport, living quarters, wages, and a safeguard of personal and political rights.[18]

Hodge reached Washington on April 22, accompanied by William Wemyss Anderson, a "silvery haired" West Indies planter and attorney retained by the BHC to draft the proposed agreement with Lincoln. In a sense, Anderson was ideally suited to the many tasks of Hodge's mission. He boasted almost three decades of involvement in the abolition movement and had been appointed by the Jamaican government in 1851 to recruit free black emigrants from North America—knowledge that would assist Hodge, a relative novice to the emigration movement. His involvement added a moral dimension to the company's business model as well. Anderson had long worked to redress the legacy of slavery in the West Indies and viewed the British colonies as an ideal location for the "education and religious instruction of the emancipated." [19]

More important, Anderson was already well known in the North American free black community. A veteran antislavery leader, he had been appointed as Jamaica's delegate to the North American Convention of Colored Freemen in Toronto, Canada, in 1851. This meeting established Anderson within the black abolitionist movement, and particularly its supporters of colonization. Along with John Scoble, the secretary of the British and Foreign Anti-Slavery Society, he addressed the gathering on the prospects of emigration to the West Indies. He also met two leading black proponents of African repatriation: fellow delegate Martin R. Delany of Pennsylvania, and Rev. Henry Highland Garnet, whose church he visited on the return trip through New York.[20] Hodge undoubtedly knew that these contacts would bolster his company's appeal to the free black population and help to shake the images of profiteering and speculation that plagued colonization.

The arrival of the pair generated modest yet encouraging enthusiasm, garnering the attention of a curious press corps that perceived another colonization scheme but could only speculate as to its design. Word of British interest in the contrabands trickled southward as well, with one Savannah newspaper describing it as a "perfect harmony" of "Yankee cunning and philanthropy, and British righteousness and self-interest." Should this new colonization scheme be adopted, the writer quipped, "the slaves will find English instead of American masters." Potential competitors took note too, with the *African Repository,* the house organ of the ACS, reporting "intelligence" of Hodge's arrival, although they misidentified him as an American.[21] Despite the brief flash of interest his arrival generated, Hodge guarded his plans until he could directly present them to Lincoln. Secrecy was a necessity in an uncertain political climate, particularly when most of the $600,000 colonization fund remained untapped.

Hodge and Anderson immediately took their credentials to Seward, receiving an atypically hearty welcome given his known skepticism toward colonization. The secretary of state must have had directions from the president himself regarding their arrival. He immediately placed the British party into contact with Usher and Senator Pomeroy, and arranged for an opportunity to present their plan directly to Lincoln. Hodge, somewhat surprisingly given the intelligence he received in London, described all he met as "favourable" to the plan and reported "so much progress that he hopes [for Lyons] to be soon in a position to request" the proclamation of the ports in a matter of weeks. At their first meeting, Lincoln initially held out for a general "convention" on British colonization through the treaty power but acceded to Hodge's suggestion that the two governments simply agree upon a common policy wherein "the emigrants would receive the same wages as others, and would be entitled to the privileges of natives." Encouraged by the presentation, Lincoln authorized Hodge to visit "contrabands camps" in Washington and Alexandria, Virginia to "ascertain if the people were willing to emigrate to Honduras."[22]

The reluctance of freed slaves to leave their country of birth severely dampened most colonization projects during the Lincoln administration, yet Hodge—undoubtedly assisted by Anderson's contacts—claimed success from his visit to the camps. "[I] found them willing provided their families were allowed to accompany them," read his report to Lyons. The enthusiasm was sufficient for Hodge to anticipate difficulty in transporting their children, who "were numerous," and at Pomeroy's suggestion, he asked Usher's department to share this cost, "which was assented to."[23] The reportedly strong response caused Hodge to request an immediate proclamation of the ports, but Lyons quickly tempered this enthusiasm by directing the BHC agent to work with Usher and present a written report on their discussions.[24]

Armed with Lincoln's verbal permission, Hodge and Anderson spent the next two weeks traveling to contraband camps and promoting the colony to leaders within the free black community. They met with a Reverend Nichols, a minister at one of the camps, and were introduced to a large contraband assembly by two colonels from the Union army, who were simultaneously recruiting soldiers from the group. Hodge also oversaw the publication of a four-page pamphlet to advertise the colony's agricultural potential and promote "the Establishment of Townships of Coloured People." He placed advertisements for the BHC project in several African American newspapers and invited prospective applicants to meet with company representatives in

Philadelphia. Encouraged by the responses they continued to receive, the company also inquired about transportation costs from shipping firms in New York.[25]

Setting up at Washington's famous Willard Hotel, the pair also presented their plan to Samuel Gridley Howe of the American Freedmen's Inquiry Commission. This committee of the War Department had been charged with investigating policies for the future of slaves freed by the Emancipation Proclamation, making it a natural point of inquiry for the colonial agents. Howe seemed interested enough for Hodge to ask for a meeting with the commission to present "the evidence we have concg. the colored race in Jamaica and Honduras." [26] Though they steered clear of official announcements pending further approval from Lincoln, Hodge and Anderson's activities sent ripples through back channels of the federal bureaucracy. James S. Mackie, an agent with the State Department, had already approached another member of the commission with information from "well informed sources" about "an English gentleman here pressing upon the attention of the authorities, a scheme for the emigration and colonization of colored people to British Honduras under the auspices of a British company."

Mackie talked up a competitor project in Spanish Honduras being promoted by his friend and fellow diplomat Ephraim G. Squier. "[I]t occurs to me that there are so many obvious reasons for preferring an American to an English enterprise," he cautioned Robert Dale Owen, a colleague of Howe. "[T]he controlling authorities need only to be acquainted with the facts to which I have adverted, to warrant them in at least *not* giving an unconditional assurance of encouragement to a Foreign Company, when the same results may be attained under purely American auspices." Assuring Owen that his motives were "unofficial," Mackie pled only an interest in ensuring the proper facts reached the commission before "our Government had compromised its faith with an association of foreign interests."[27] Such was the competitive nature of colonization politics, where rival schemes constantly emerged to claim their stake of the $600,000 appropriation, even if it meant discouraging alternative emigration locales.

Hodge dispatched Anderson to Philadelphia in May, where the latter gave a lecture about the "social and spiritual condition of [British Honduras'] coloured inhabitants" at the Sixth Street Bethel Chapel. "In this country," he told the audience, "the people of color are not a nation—not a people—but outsiders." The former slaves of the United States could find acceptance and employment though in the British colonies, which "will pay the expenses of such as have small families desiring to go there." While his speech was received with much praise, a correspondent in attendance presciently remarked upon the "unfavorable" timing of the address in light of the War Department's efforts to recruit black soldiers. "After the termination of this war, there will, we think, be a better opportunity presented to get laborers to go to that country, whether they go with the intention of remaining or not."[28]

Anderson proceeded next to New York to deliver a similar presentation at the Shiloh Presbyterian Church, an influential black congregation and an organization point for the Underground Railroad. It was here that the BHC crossed paths with Rev. Henry Highland Garnet, an old acquaintance who eventually became one of the project's primary supporters within the black community. Born into slavery, Garnet escaped at a young age to New York where he became a fiery abolitionist preacher and an early proponent of African repatriation. Anderson again reported a favorable audience, receiving the thanks of Garnet who also directed the church organist to play "God Save the Queen" in his honor.[29]

It is possible that Hodge and Anderson's recruitment efforts first brought them into acquaintance with another African American supporter, J. Willis Menard. Born in 1838 to a free black Creole family in Illinois, Menard was already an accomplished abolitionist pamphleteer by his early twenties, as well as a widely acclaimed poet for several African American newspapers. He established himself in the early 1860s as one of the nation's most prominent colonizationists within the free black community through a series of public exchanges with Frederick Douglass, a colonization critic.[30] Mitchell recruited Menard to assist in the Lincoln administration's colonization projects by hiring him as a clerk in early 1863.[31] He initially investigated proposals sent to the Emigration Office from Liberia, but Hodge's presentation appealed to him, and he began assisting Mitchell on the West Indies project.

Rumors of Hodge's encouraging response also reached the government of Guiana, spawned by favorable reports to Dickson from Mitchell. Walker's appointed agent checked in with the British Legation on May 11, requesting notification should the prospects improve for Guiana's participation in the emigration scheme. Lyons apprised him of Hodge's "progress" but urged patience until a formal agreement was concluded, assuring him that its results would not favor Honduras over Guiana.[32]

On May 7, Hodge presented Usher with a report of his findings from the contraband camps and submitted preliminary terms for a cost-sharing agreement with the U.S. government, fully expecting its impending approval based on the secretary's earlier assurances. The BHC agreed to finance the transport of 500 to 1,000 adult male laborers and their spouses, while the United States would bear the cost for an estimated 1,500 to 3,000 children and elderly dependents.[33] The colonization fund still contained well in excess of $500,000, and Usher's intimations led Britain to believe a portion of it would soon be released for the project. Having received favorable signals from the legation, Hodge also anticipated the Foreign Office's sanction of contraband recruits so long as they were transported through the northern ports. This initial contract would serve as the foundation for a larger plan of "Self-Sustaining Emigration," designed by Anderson with the legation's input, wherein the United States would provide seed money for the transport of 5,000 laborers annually over the next ten years. The proposed contract obliged colonists to apply their earnings to this fund for a fixed period. In exchange, the indenture came with a contractual assurance of land ownership upon repayment.[34]

Negotiations concluded on May 9 with all expectations that an agreement would soon be announced, as Hodge enthusiastically reported back to Lyons.[35] Yet in only two days' time, the previous several months' work would seem for naught, and the project stood on the brink of collapse. On May 11 Usher inexplicably changed his mind. The scheme would advance no further, its requests having become "inexpedient" and the vaguely hinted-at circumstances of the Interior Department's changing colonization policies having made it not "worth the while to discuss the particular terms of the proposition submitted by you." Usher's letter exhibited an uncharacteristic lawyerly tone, cloaked with nuance and discouraging of further inquiry into the cause. Though Britain was finally warming to Lincoln's long-sought inclusion of the contrabands, Usher now deemed them off-limits. He explained that the colonization fund was "limited to those free blacks resident within D.C. as at April 1862" or freed in July by the Confiscation Act, namely contrabands, but neither category would be accessible to the BHC. The labor "most desired by the British Honduras Company, viz. the able-bodied males, are now engaged in making arrangements to enlist in a different enterprise, from which it is not deemed politic to divert them." Furthermore, "in the opinion of the Secretary of War," Hodge would no longer be permitted to even visit the contraband camps.[36]

Plainly frustrated by this unforeseen turn of events, Hodge had reason to believe himself the victim of political intrigue. Usher's about-face seemed to defy every prior signal from the secretary or his department, not to mention the instructions received directly from Lincoln. Unknown to Britain, the responsible party was Edwin McMasters Stanton, the cantankerous secretary of war and a recurring cause of intracabinet agitation.

Though Union officers at the camps welcomed the British agents, word of Hodge's visits irritated Stanton, who viewed the company as competition for the recruitment of black enlistees. Usher had apparently snubbed Hodge at Stanton's behest, the May 11 letter being subjected to the secretary of war's personal edits.[37]

The interior secretary's conversion to Stanton's position is more difficult to understand, as he expressed early support for the project and even remained nominally sympathetic to colonization after this point. Control of the colonization fund appears a likely culprit, as the British plan involved Mitchell's Emigration Office and accordingly expanded its budgetary oversight. The secretary's predecessor Caleb Smith routinely approved Mitchell's discretionary spending and additions to his staff, but Usher resented Mitchell's impatience with department protocol. Seward's leisurely approach to the negotiations created many opportunities for Mitchell to initiate his own communications with Lyons, an act viewed by Usher as insubordination.

Hodge, desperate as his work unraveled before him, pled his case to Seward and, apparently, any other administration official who would listen. As the contrabands enlisting in the army would primarily be young men, "the remaining labourers must necessarily be family men" with wives and children and, thus, presumably unaffected by Stanton's policy. He also appealed directly to the social status of blacks after emancipation. British Honduras was willing to offer them "social, religious and political rights . . . already secured by law," a condition they were unlikely to find in other colonial locations or, indeed, the United States itself.[38] Hodge also sent a final plea to Usher on May 14, by requesting only "two or three hundred able-bodied labourers." He sought the reinstatement of his privilege to visit the camps, "so readily and graciously acceded to me by His Excellency the President." When no response came, the British agent resigned himself to accepting his mission's failure and confided as much to Lyons.[39] On May 17 the *New York Times* reported that Hodge "was so strongly opposed by the Secretary of War . . . that the mission failed, and the gentleman went home."[40] Though Stanton was indeed the instigator, the *Times* reached this conclusion prematurely. Hodge possessed a trump card from an unexpected source.

Usher's change of opinion slighted members of his own government, and Hodge quickly found friends in the administration who were eager to help him circumvent the War Department's roadblock. Mitchell, who had restructured his office in anticipation of the project, urged Hodge to press forward, as did Postmaster General Montgomery Blair, leader of the cabinet's colonization faction. Always eager to irritate the Radical Republicans in Congress, Blair took it upon himself to preach the administration's commitment to separating the races by colonization though he often did so without Lincoln's tact. Blair likely had Hodge's difficulties in mind on May 20 as he gave a widely disseminated speech about Lincoln's emancipation policy. He characterized the contraband camps as a preparatory staging ground for colonization after the war, whereupon the military value of the freedmen would cease. "Under proper discipline they will here learn much to fit them for self-government as an independent people, associated with a kindred race that now invites them to a congenial climate and a soil rich in all the productions best suited to repay in commerce the nations of more advanced civilization, for the protection and assistance they may have given them in their new homes with the governments into which they are admitted."[41]

In conclusion, Blair assured his audience that the "destined glory" of the freedmen "is to be consummated in the American tropics" where they will be "aided with the capital and intelligence of the great commercial powers," undoubtedly a reference to the British Empire.[42] The speech was as much a rejoinder to Stanton as an expression of its stated function, the extolling of Lincoln's Emancipation Proclamation before the public, still uneasy with its racial implications. Blair viewed the secretary of war with suspicion and contempt long before this episode though and, according to the War Department's Assistant Secretary Charles A. Dana, Stanton returned those feelings.[43] As he plastered the War Department with a public broadside, Blair also itched to display his personal influence with Lincoln. Hodge's troubles provided such an opportunity, and not long after Usher's slighting the BHC agent received a "voluntary offer of one of the Cabinet" to escape the War Department's impediment.[44]

At some point in late May, Hodge met with Blair and Mitchell to revamp the BHC offer and present it to the president.[45] Mitchell, confident of obtaining Lincoln's support, took Hodge's proposal to Seward and asked that the project be jointly considered with Walker's 1862 plan for Guiana. Both schemes fulfilled the stipulations of the September 30 circular to Adams, and the emigration commissioner believed he could make the British Honduras offer more attractive by convincing Hodge to finance the scheme without federal subsidy. An appeal to London's economic interests in a successful crop "may cause them to expend direct aid to the colonies in this work." Time was against them due to the growing season. No sensible investor would allow vast tracts of land to sit idle for lack of workers, even if he had to advance their transportation cost. Hodge was "reluctant to abandon his claims to pecuniary aid," but after Mitchell's pressing he consented and traveled to New York for an arranged meeting with Dickson. The two drafted a "uniform proposition" governing emigration in both colonies, intending to elude the secretary of war's opposition with a politically palatable appeal to the president.[46]

The revamped proposal portended a significant shift in the administration's colonization strategy, though it also continued the course that Lincoln had laid before Congress in late 1862, *sans* a treaty component. Colonization would no longer depend upon a contractual obligation between the government and private recipients of federal funding. Rather, by simple agreement the United States would permit and encourage designated colonial landholders to recruit black laborers, albeit with loose oversight from the Emigration Office. With Hodge's assent, the United States had convinced Britain to finance the scheme in its entirety save for the anticipated employment of agents in Mitchell's office to assist with the recruitment.

Hodge's concession of funding was not atypical for the colonial West Indies, which subsidized the import of laborers from China and India across much greater distances. The comparatively short voyage from the North American mainland would, in fact, be a welcome means of cutting his company's transportation costs. Stanton's political obstructions provided a more immediate pretext for this shift in the project's funding, though it was also one that Lincoln was likely to welcome for other reasons. Aside from the obvious budgetary enticement, it probably reflected American weariness of the dodgy speculators who had flocked to the colonization fund the previous year. Also Mitchell could carry the project through without depending on Usher's approval for large expenditures from the colonization fund.

Hodge returned to Washington on June 10 and received word from Usher that Stanton remained adamantly opposed to recruitment among the contrabands or in the District of Columbia. Furthermore, as these were the only categories covered by Congress's appropriation, the Interior Department could not assist him in the colonization of other free blacks.[47] These terms made the 1862 colonization laws inoperable, their funds strictly confined to the categories of blacks in which Stanton would permit no recruitment. Perhaps feeling a sense of guilt over his prior assurances to the BHC, Usher completely disavowed his earlier complicity with Stanton and blamed this paradoxical situation entirely on War Department policies that were beyond his control. Hodge remained courteous with the secretary but was moved to circumvent him by the futility of further appeals to his department. "[S]eeing that I must either accept it or abandon my object for the present," he consented to Blair's offer to "remove the difficulty" created by Stanton. Hodge's scheme fell well beyond the purview of the postmaster general's official duties, but it stood in accord with his personal views. Blair presented Hodge's dilemma to Lincoln and, finding the president supportive, arranged for a private meeting at the White House.[48]

When Hodge arrived on June 13, he found Lincoln holding an order that encompassed his "uniform proposition" with Dickson, placed under the guidance of Mitchell's office:

> Emigration Office
> Washington D.C. June 11th, 1863
>
> John Hodge of London, and S. R. Dickson, agents of the British Colonies of Honduras and Guiana, are here in accordance with the well settled policy of the United States, to aid such free persons of color as desire to remove to their colonies. We, therefore, recommend all parties and persons having the direction or charge of such, to present no hindrance to them or their agents in the work of canvassing for emigrants, but to render them and their regularly appointed agents, all the aid possible in this work.
>
> James Mitchell
> *Commissioner of Emigration*[49]

He then presented Lincoln with Usher's May 11 letter dismissing the project. Lincoln reviewed his subordinate's decision then, turning to Hodge, "said that what he had told me at first was his honest desire." The emigration of free blacks would proceed. Next, wrote Hodge in his report to Lyons, "he handed me the authority which had been drawn up by the Govt. Emigration Commissioner, signed by himself" with the dated endorsement, "I approve the within."[50]

The project now bore Lincoln's written sanction, but Stanton continued to impede. Not long after the meeting Mitchell "carried the papers conferring the privilege to the War Department for Secretary Stanton's action. The secretary wrote on them: 'Not approved.'" According to Mitchell, Stanton's refusal so infuriated Lincoln that the emigration commissioner withdrew the War Department's answer from the president's sight, promising that time would soften this act of insubordination. Mitchell later recalled the incident as being one of only two times he ever saw Lincoln lose his temper.[51]

To Hodge, Lincoln's authorization provided a welcome reversal of fortunes and cause for immediate proclamation of the ports. The BHC could prepare its lands for colonists as the Americans ironed out the remaining administrative issues. He urged Lyons to transmit word of his success on the next ship from New York to Belize City. With a little luck, Seymour would be able to declare the ports in time for the next growing season. "When last in Washington I could have got several hundred of contraband and other emigrants," he continued, and "I trust . . . to obtain sufficient to fill a vessel before long" for their transport.[52]

Chapter 4

The Contrabands Question

Lyons met Hodge's exuberance over Lincoln's answer with characteristic cynicism. As he complained to Russell, Lincoln had a habit "of approving papers submitted by subordinates, without coming to an understanding with his Cabinet." He sent Hodge to New York to locate Usher. Humbled by Lincoln's order, the secretary conceded "that as the President had given his sanction he was agreeable to it." Lyons deemed Hodge's "progress" sufficient to authorize the long-awaited port proclamation and requested Seward's prompt assent in order to send word to Seymour "by a vessel which is on the point of sailing."[1]

The contrabands issue, long dormant and seemingly appeased by limiting canvassers to northern ports, suddenly reemerged as a source of diplomatic worry. Lyons privately told Russell that he "should very much like to get as many 'Contrabands' as possible safe out of this Country," fearing for their welfare in a postwar United States. "The question is too large a one for me to pretend to settle," given its political implications for Britain's position on the war. Thus, Lyons requested direction from London before permitting Hodge to canvass from this class of people. Russell found himself "disposed to agree" with Lyons's apprehension and halted the proclamation of the ports, even if the Americans acceded to the plan.[2]

The Foreign Office's retraction ignited an internal war of words with the Colonial Office, which considered the issue settled and instructed Hodge to negotiate around that assumption, provided he confine recruitment to northern cities. Hodge has "overcome all difficulties of detail," complained one Colonial Office letter to Russell's secretary, only to have "found himself at the last moment debarred." Hodge protested the decision to Lyons as well, stating that Lincoln intended the inclusion of contrabands in his order. He solicited and obtained a clarification from Mitchell as to whether the order's wording, "free persons of color," included contrabands. Attorney

General Bates advised that "there is no distinction in law it is only in time," indicating the contrabands could be included.[3]

Frustrated by the latest legal hurdle and content to allow its resolution through the Colonial and Foreign Office bureaucracies, Hodge sailed for Belize on July 11. He informed Lyons of his intent to "wait until I hear all obstructions to the emigration have been removed" and return at a more opportune time in the future. The BHC encountered some difficulty recruiting laborers from the free black population of the North, as the wages most received in the United States exceeded what the BHC could offer. Hodge nonetheless reported finding a "general belief" among the black population "that the whites intend to separate the races after the war now raging." Many are now "ascertain[ing] the best places for future homes," a decision that the BHC hoped to encourage with the speedy resolution of the contrabands issue.[4]

The Colonial Office lodged a vigorous objection with Russell over the exclusion of the contrabands. With another growing season slipping by, Newcastle saw the urgent need for agricultural laborers in the West Indies. One letter complained that the entire emigration policy's success depended upon the contrabands, the largest intended group of recruits. It was "certainly assumed on both sides that such an emigration was not objectionable in principle, provided it was confined to northern ports."[5] Newcastle found the Foreign Office's reasons for caution unconvincing, particularly given the Confederacy's growing military troubles. "There is no United States law to prevent these persons from leaving New York or Boston, there is no colonial law to prevent their arrival at Belize." As his assistant secretary contended,

> It would seem to be a question whether Her Majesty's Government are bound contrary to the desire of the United States Government to exercise a superintendence over British emigrant ships in United States ports, and to examine into the previous history of the emigrants, in order to ascertain that none of them are refugees from the Confederate States. And it would appear to be a sufficient answer to any representation on the subject from the authorities of those states, that the emigration was conducted from Federal ports by private individuals, and that Her Majesty's Government interfered in the matter no further than to secure the proper treatment of the emigrants without considering themselves bound to enquire whether they had or had not escaped, or been driven by necessity from the southern states.[6]

Newcastle's arguments ultimately prevailed upon Russell, who drafted a notice to Lyons on August 5, reversing his decision yet again. "I waive all objections to the class of coloured persons called 'contrabands' being included in the emigration provided it is strictly confined to the northern ports."[7] For Newcastle's purposes, the port proclamation could proceed. Lyons waited only for the American State Department's approval.

Seward did little to advance the scheme while the contrabands issue preoccupied his British counterpart. Nor did he likely want to, given his personal opposition to colonization. With Lincoln's policy now defined per the meeting with Hodge, what was once casual inattention cloaked in the natural sluggishness of negotiation now suggested deliberate inertia on the part of the secretary. Notwithstanding near daily communication with the British Legation and despite the urgency attached to the original letter, the State Department did not send its acknowledgment of Lyons's June 17 request on the port proclamation for almost two months. The answer arrived unexpectedly on August 10, finally giving the United States government's sanction to proceed:

> My Lord: In your note of the 17th of June last, which has been received, your lordship inquires whether it would be agreeable to this government if a proclamation should be made by the governor of British Honduras under the provisions of an act of the legislature of that colony, declaring that Boston, New York, and Philadelphia are regarded as ports of emigration, with a view to canvass for an emigration of colored laborers from the United States.
>
> Having taken the directions of the President, I have to inform your lordship that this government interposes no objection to the voluntary immigration of persons of the class described, and of course none to the proclamation proposed.[8]

What prompted Seward's sudden consent after months of inaction is necessarily speculative, though James Mitchell left some clues. In all probability the secretary of state spent the intervening months attempting to sway Lincoln's mind against the scheme. At an August 18 meeting, Lincoln told Mitchell that Seward approached him a few days prior with "a paper . . . unfavorable to the British requests for colonists," seeking his authorization. "I did not want to do so," continued Lincoln, "but asked him to leave the paper with me. I wrote out the form of an answer myself and sent it to the State Department," apparently directing them to approve the "English

Propositions." At the same meeting Mitchell reportedly asked Lincoln if "colonization was still the policy of the Administration." The president answered in the affirmative, stressing that "such scenes as those in New York the other day, where negroes were hanged to lamp posts" during the draft riots had reinforced his conviction. "It would have been much better to separate the races."[9]

Clearly encouraged by Lincoln's comments, Mitchell spent the next day composing articles to announce the impending commencement of black migration to the British colonies. In a column for the *Methodist* newspaper, he wrote that an agreement had been reached with the British government under the "sanction of the President" to transport volunteer laborers from the free black population to the British West Indies. A similar article in the *New York Observer* announced that the plan "will go into effect so soon as the State Department has fully adjusted the matter with the British minister."[10]

As per the articles, Mitchell prepared his office to receive canvassers from the British colonies, whom he would then assist with recruitment and transportation. "Be so good as to grant me a statement of the condition of the negotiations with the British Minister," he wrote the State Department on September 15. Should Seward require further information, Mitchell intimated, he need only consult the American consular agents in the colonies, as they had been kept apprised of the BHC's projects.[11]

Despite Hodge's successes and the resolution of the contrabands issue, the call for emigrants still lacked the desired response within the free black population. Mitchell had a plan to stimulate that interest though, and as the Emigration Office prepared the public to receive the latest colonization scheme through the press, its clerk J. Willis Menard waited out the month-long voyage from New York to Belize City with Hodge.[12]

Chapter 5

This Most Desirable Country

The *Antonio Mathe* was a "small but stanch brig." Captained by C. H. Stephens and with an officer's complement of two, she sailed a mail route between New York and Belize City. The Caribbean hurricane season made summer voyages unpredictable and potentially treacherous for such a modest vessel. Departing July 11, she made a particularly stormy run and arrived in British Honduras twenty-eight days later. The ship's cabins were sparse even by the day's standard, but the small crew "did all in their power" to make their passengers comfortable during the voyage.[1]

On board the *Mathe* were John Hodge, manager of the colony's most powerful land corporation, and four guests of the company, "three colored men and one white," who came to bear witness to the proposed colony at Hodge's invitation.[2] The BHC-financed tour was a gamble from the outset. They departed amidst the uncertainty of the contrabands dispute and had no knowledge of its resolution while they were at sea. The identities of the party's members are only partially known, though they styled themselves "commissioners" and made varying impressions on Charles Leas, the U.S. consul, who greeted them upon arrival. One man was a Canadian, and the other three Americans. Two of the men were lawyers, accused by Leas of having succumbed to the "temptation of large personal advantages providing they will return to the states and bring with them a body of emigrants." The other two, Leas noted, "are men of hand-fisted honesty, and will look at the whole question as its merits demand."[3]

J. Willis Menard led the delegation as a representative of the Emigration Office and intended spokesman to the contrabands, should the prohibition be lifted. Traveling with him was another young man named Charles Babcock of Salem, Massachusetts, variously described as a "mulatto" with part Narraganset Indian heritage who "identifies himself with the colored people and their interests."[4] Menard and Babcock had met some years prior while working with Rev. Henry Highland Garnet's African Civilization

Society. Like Menard, Babcock initially saw Liberia as the key to the African race's future but had come to view the Caribbean as an equally suited and geographically closer point of migration.[5]

Little else is known about the other two "commissioners." The Canadian, a black preacher who went by the name Mr. Keef, had been sent by an unnamed Baptist congregation as part of a two-member "deputation," but the other man had taken sick shortly before their departure.[6] The identity and purpose of the party's Caucasian member is lost to history.

On the day of their arrival Hodge introduced his delegation to Leas and also provided the consulate with a copy of a BHC pamphlet describing the proposed colony.[7] The group spent several days in Belize City where Hodge hosted them at the BHC's land office and presented them to several colonial government officials. The men were impressed to see an all-black Zouave unit guarding the town's small defensive garrison, Fort George. Somewhat astonished, Babcock wrote of the abundance of commercial goods in the town's market, including "all the Yankee Notions" that "can be had nearly as cheap" as in the United States. They inspected the legislative assembly building, visited several churches, and greeted the local inhabitants, finding them "quite hospitable" and willing to shelter the American party as the town lacked any regular hotels or boardinghouses.[8]

Hodge arranged for the group to be accompanied on a tour of the planting region by John Roles, described as "an old Louisiana cotton planter" and "thorough abolitionist" who sought wage laborers "of whatever shade of complection" [*sic*] for his farm. They traveled eighty miles north along the coast where they encountered J. H. Blake, Esq. a "gentleman of color" who operated a hundred-acre cotton plantation in the region. The party continued on to the BHC's tract of land along the New River Lagoon, site of the proposed colony. The site was already being subdivided into farms and prepared for settlement. Back in Belize City, Hodge explained the company's plans to Seymour and informed him that the New River site already contained five hundred acres of land sown with cotton. Babcock took notice of the northern region's fertility, seeing "plenty of sugar cane, cotton, corn, and tobacco" in the early stages of cultivation. Next the party traveled inland through mahogany country to observe the production techniques then returned to Belize City by way of the coast.[9]

The Americans took careful notes on the colony's economy and social structure. Medicine was hard to come by, "save the famous snake doctor, of which every community has one." Babcock considered this a sign of a lack of demand for physicians, though, a condition he attributed to the low population density and a climate that he actually considered more favorable to his health than the cold winters of New England. The population consisted of indigenous persons and a large "Creole" demographic—a broad designation that included "all shades of complexion, from that of an unmixed descendant of the former African slave" to mulattoes and the "unmixed Creole, born of white parents." The English numbered approximately 150, yet comprised the ruling class—a disparity that struck Babcock "quite forcibly." He nonetheless praised the relations between the races, which were free of "hostile prejudices . . . so far as *color* is concerned." The visible disparity of property ownership caused some unease, particularly since the BHC advertised the widespread availability of land. Babcock echoed Leas's correspondence from the previous February in which he stressed the need for safeguards against low wages and the economic exploitation of the laboring class. He nonetheless saw promise in the BHC's willingness to divide the New River Lagoon tract into small parcels for purchase or rent by emigrants.[10]

At the time of the group's visit Belize had less than a hundred registered voters and a relatively low suffrage qualification threshold based on annual income or land ownership. Race, however, was not a disqualifier to political participation, and, in fact, the colony's attorney general, three court justices, eight members of the twenty-one-seat legislature, and several administrative officers were black. Babcock found the colony's small population advantageous for attaining political clout. He asked potential colonists to compare it "with other places we have been asked to emigrate" and recognize the probability of "soon becoming a political power in the colony."[11]

The four "commissioners" parted ways in early September, with each expressing his liking of the colony, albeit with stipulations and expectations for the BHC to fulfill. Housing was a must, as with the promise of eventual land-ownership opportunities. Babcock, Menard, and the third unnamed gentleman departed for the United States by different routes, intending to disseminate information about the colony to the black community. The commencement of colonization also appeared imminent, as Governor Seymour officially proclaimed the ports of Boston, New York, and Philadelphia on September 17.[12]

The fourth member of the party, Keef of Canada, was apparently "delighted" with the tropical climate's effects on his health and decided to remain. He purchased a tract of cotton land on a coastal island and announced his intent to send for his family in short order with funds raised from the first year's crop. Babcock travelled to Jamaica before eventually catching a steamer to Boston in October or November. Menard departed directly for New York, arriving in a few weeks. From Hodge's perspective, the delegation served its purpose of introducing the colony to leaders within the free black community. A contributor to the British Anti-Slavery Society's newspaper, the *Anti-Slavery Reporter,* also took notice of the visit. They came "seeking information respecting this country as a place to emigrate to" and departed with satisfaction, bearing Hodge's offers to prospective recruits in hand.[13]

Word of the delegation's successes first reached the United States around September 16, when Menard's ship reached New York. He immediately began disseminating information about the colony within the northern free black community. An African American newspaper in Philadelphia interviewed the Emigration Office clerk and found that he "expressed himself as being highly pleased with Honduras." He nonetheless cautioned against initiating a massive emigration at the time "for want of proper necessaries and facilities on their arrival." Instead, migration should occur with only "a few at a time, of the right stamp."[14]

Menard also called upon Rev. Henry Highland Garnet and delivered a presentation at the Shiloh Presbyterian Church about his recent "visit to Honduras." As noted, Garnet knew of the scheme already, having hosted one of Anderson's lectures in June.[15] Garnet's own near-death experience during the summer's draft riots had rejuvenated his interest in African repatriation, making the British Honduras project a welcome and timely appeal. For this same reason Menard's talk resonated with others in the congregation.

Junius C. Morel, a prominent member of the church and a Brooklyn-based newspaper correspondent, noted the effect of the riots within the black community in his eyewitness account of the violence. "Many are casting about and considering the propriety of emigration to the British West Indies, where they may raise their children and fe[e]l that they are men in the eyes of the law, with all due protection. These repeated discouragements which we have been receiving from the hands of the dominant class in these cities have well nigh satisfied us that there is no real safety for person or property belonging to us."[16] Following Menard's talk, Morel himself joined this call and urged his readers to better their condition "by being the owner of one hundred acres of good, rich, productive soil in Honduras."[17]

The African Civilization Society began its own preparations to assist with emigration to the New River Lagoon colony. The society had associated with the colonization movement since its founding by Garnet in 1859, though its primary function was to provide charitable and educational services to the black community. Like many in the black colonizationist movement, Garnet's organization straddled the fence between the divergent objectives of encouraging blacks' emigration abroad and bettering their condition in the United States. The organization lent its support to Martin R. Delany's investigations of Liberia and the Niger Valley in 1859 and maintained an office in New York City's Bible House building alongside the New York Colonization Society. Domestically, it organized a network of schools for freedmen and the contrabands of the war. By 1863 though, Garnet himself was vacillating between emigration and encouraging recruitment for the United States Colored Troops.

The society's views on emigration changed over the years, most notably in 1861 when Delany proposed an amendment to its charter. One article asserted that "[t]he Society is not designed to encourage general emigration," holding that its participants must be "practically qualified" persons who would promote Christian morals and the improvement of the African race abroad. This addendum likely reflected Delany's frustrations with his previous African ventures, where a dearth of skilled laborer volunteers and troubles with white missionaries and warring tribal chiefs derailed his plans for establishing the modern "Black Israel" vision of his earlier career. A second plank nonetheless deemed emigration consistent with the society's goals and encouraged the continued search for an African homeland: "The basis of the Society, and ulterior objects in encouraging emigration shall be: Self Reliance and Self Government on the principle of an African Nationality, the African race being the ruling element of the nation, controlling and directing their own affairs."[18]

In one sense, the society's embrace of the British Honduras project represents a deviation from the traditional interpretation of the group's changing attitudes on emigration. The 1861 amendments seemed to signal a domestic turn in its mission, perhaps best summarized by a speaker at their May 1863 meeting: "We have, indeed, been hindered from planting our standard on African soil, but happily our constitution is universal in its language and spirit." Finding that the "African door was shut," they turned to the condition of blacks in the United States. This changing outlook took hold within the black abolitionist community in the wake of emancipation and the enlistment of black troops. Even Menard, long among the most vocal supporters of Liberian migration, conceded that he was torn between resettlement abroad and working to improve the lot of blacks at home.[19] But by summer's end, with the draft riots in immediate hindsight, the search for a suitable foreign location was back on the society's agenda. On September 5, a general meeting of the society appointed a new committee on the "British Provinces, in the American tropics" to be chaired by Garnet himself.[20] As occasionally occurred in the black-repatriation and white-colonization movements, the British Honduras colony had produced an unlikely political alliance between black and white leaders with widely divergent racial views and motives.

J. Willis Menard wrote Lincoln from New York before returning to Washington. He promised to provide the president with a detailed report of the mission and requested funds for its publication in pamphlet form "for general distribution among my race."[21] There is no indication if Lincoln acted on Menard's request, and though Menard reportedly compiled a summary of the mission's findings for the president it does not appear to have survived.[22] He did, however, commit a brief description of his travels to verse:

> Twas on a morning like this that I were to set out, with a skillful band of explorers,
> For the far-off western hills and dales in the vernal wilds of Honduras.
> After freighting our proud and restless boat, with luggage, provisions, utensils,
> We spread her snowy wings to the wind, and sailed up the coast of Honduras![23]

Fortunately another record of this forgotten investigative mission survived. Charles Babcock published a report of his own in early November 1863 for distribution to potential emigrants. Babcock unhesitatingly declared his support for the project. "All able-bodied, energetic, industrious colored men with their families, and a small capital, emigrating to the colony of British Honduras, *cannot fail of success*." The pamphlet circulated widely among free blacks in the north and even gained a favorable review in William Lloyd Garrison's *The Liberator*.[24]

Even after the visit of Menard and his delegation, the U.S. Consulate in Belize City looked upon the project with suspicion. Leas was not opposed to colonization *per se*, in fact, quite the contrary. In November 1863 he sent the State Department an elaborately opinionated manuscript of several hundred pages in length, apparently hoping the government would publish it as a "History of British Honduras." The better part of a chapter contains his personal assessment of colonization. He described the BHC plan as an "honorable" one but said it was also "mistaken" for allegedly replicating the plantation system of Jamaica at the expense of the colonists. With perhaps equal significance, he feared an ill-conceived project that would overburden the consulate as destitute colonists sought passage back to the United States. Though Hodge assured him this would not be the case, Leas attached his own interests to the colonization discussions at the State Department. He volunteered an alternate scheme of his own design in which the government parceled out individual farms of a couple of acres apiece. Should this option replace the "hasty and inconsiderate immigration" he initially perceived in the BHC's plans, he would offer his personal, not to mention effusive, endorsement. The freedmen, he predicted, would soon "seek this country as their future home, flowering as it naturally does, with 'milk and honey.'"[25]

With time, Hodge's continued presence in the colony went a long way toward alleviating Leas's misgivings about the British Honduras Company, as it defied the consul's experiences with other London landowners who managed their properties and laborers from a distance. Leas never completely warmed to the New River Lagoon site, though he eventually found that he could better the arrangements for the American freedmen by working directly with the company. In late October shipboard whispers reached the U.S. consulate about some "two hundred families of colored people" in New York waiting "in readiness to emigrate to this country." Initially skeptical due to the "trouble and annoyance" caused to him by prior colonization speculators, Leas called upon Hodge to verify the rumor.[26]

Leas's sources were indeed reliable. A BHC canvasser in New York had been "in correspondence with the Rev. Mr. Garnett" [*sic*], who was encouraging the recruitment of colonists along with Menard and Babcock. Hodge instructed his agent to "engage a steamer, if at all, on moderate terms and send them down upon the conditions" laid out in the company's printed circulars. In addition to transit, the group would receive one thousand dollars of the company's funds to secure a minister to travel with them, as well as a "good medical gentleman."[27]

Around the same time the BHC approached the British government with an application for a contract to run a mail steamer from Belize to New York City. This was likely no coincidence, as the establishment of such routes, which had been something of a craze in the U.S. during the early 1850s, had often been justified by hopes that they might achieve other goals and pay for themselves in the long run. The mail routes would increase communication with, and thus the commercial penetration of, distant parts of the world. They also provided ships that might be converted to naval use in times of war or indeed one day might carry emigrants from the United States. The American Colonization Society was always angling for such a route to Liberia, and in 1850 many deportation-inclined politicians threw their weight behind the campaign for an "Ebony Line" to help African Americans on their way. The ACS's efforts were in vain, and the whole speculative idea of the value of mail steamers had been dealt a blow in Congress due to southern ire and budgetary retrenchment by the late 1850s, but the association of steamer contracts with the movement of people was an obvious one. As to Belize, William Heriot of the BHC told Whitehall that there had been increased trade with New York since its recent promotion to the status of colony. Commerce was likely to grow yet further with the agricultural production brought about by the prospective importation of American laborers.[28] But in all likelihood he was thinking about how to introduce such people in the first place, too.

Two months had passed since the State Department gave its approval to the port proclamation through Lincoln's direct intervention, but Seward continued to progress at a snail's pace. As of October 25, Leas "had received no instructions . . . in regard to the matter of emigration." Absent this direction, the consul took it upon himself to secure proper living arrangements for the anticipated colonists lest they arrive in squalor and "crowd this agency office for relief and assistance." Hodge assured Leas that the colonists would be well attended with a dwelling space for each family. The company secured a shipment of lumber for the "construction of houses with wood floors, windows, and elevated three feet from the ground." Building materials for future houses would be cut on-site at a sawmill also under construction and intended as a place of employment for the initial wave of laborers. Lastly, the company would budget "$500 per annum for educational purposes."[29]

Mindful of their prior arrangements, Hodge asked the Emigration Office to assist his agents with the proposed group of colonists. He apprised Mitchell of the construction project that would soon be under way "on the banks of the New River Lagoon, which Menard knows well and can describe to you." The colony needed workers who knew the techniques of farming, as well as mechanics to operate the sawmill machinery. Belize had only recently gotten word of the contrabands issue's resolution, though Hodge knew he was still in competition with the War Department for this valuable labor source. As he wrote Mitchell, "I hope before long you will manage to send me" emigrants from this class. "It is the Contrabands that I depend upon to hire as good continuous laborers, for those from the North will be chiefly on their own account as small farmers" though "[t]hey however will be excellent pioneers to draw others after them."[30]

Economic interests undoubtedly lurked behind the BHC's promises and rhetoric, and Leas was quick to point them out. He was also quick to stress any aspect of Hodge's plan that might burden his own office with emigration papers to process, particularly at the behest of a for-profit enterprise. The company, though enjoying extensive privilege from the British government, was created for the purpose of land speculation. They intended to engage the colonists in a large agricultural venture much as Jamaica had done with its black population after full emancipation reached that island in 1838. To this end, Hodge entertained virtually every possible means of obtaining labor from the United States. Reflecting both his company's flexibility and, perhaps, his personal naivete in pursuit of an economic goal, Hodge openly wondered whether white southern planters eventually might be enticed to the colony as well, where they could impart their knowledge of cotton plantation management and adapt it to a free-labor system.[31]

It would be overly simplistic to reduce the project's motives to profit alone. Leas, while a skeptic, took comfort in the favorable resolution of the contrabands issue. Britain, he wrote Seward, had "at last regarded the reclaimatory pronouncements of the Davis Junta as but an *ignis fatuus.*" Despite his clear business motive, Hodge, too, genuinely adhered to abolitionist beliefs and took great care to ensure their representation in his company through antislavery movement veterans such as Anderson. "Destroy slavery, and you will kill the power of Slave Masters," he told Mitchell, and in that enterprise "I shall aid all I can." Like Russell, he recognized that the recruitment of the contrabands would antagonize the Confederacy. He had little use for diplomatic neutrality with the South, though, and praised this eventual authorization as England's stand "against any supposed claims of the Confederates for their escaped slaves."[32]

Rushed for time to meet the approaching crop season, the British agents announced a ship would be leaving New York in December "so as to arrive in that period, named the dry season here, the most healthy for those not acclimated."[33] Encouraging reports from London and New York prompted Hodge to again solicit Mitchell's assistance in the recruitment effort. In a brief reply, the emigration commissioner informed him that preparations for the project were still under way and "the President is disposed to sustain it against all unfriendly influences."[34] The administration still lacked political unity behind the project though, and far from the interested parties gaining direction after Lincoln's intervention with Seward in August, the divisions between them were deepening. Unknown to Hodge, Seward had kept the Interior Department waiting for over two months before sending formal notification of his letter to Lyons authorizing the port proclamations.[35] It was neither the first nor the last instance in which the secretary of state passively impeded colonization through simple inaction. By January 1864, the long-discussed transport ship still existed only on paper with no clear indication of its future from the American authorities.

From the Belizean point of view, however, the failure of the exodus appeared attributable not to American factors, but rather to an unexpected event on December 13, 1863. Whitehall suddenly changed its mind on the contrabands again and, offering little explanation, ordered the governor of Jamaica to prohibit "any action to be taken as yet for the introduction of Negroes from the United States into British Honduras."[36] The absence of protest in the sources suggests that Hodge and the BHC took the blow and moved on, which is perhaps not so surprising given how many times the project appeared to have been on the verge of collapse; even in October, Hodge's letter to Mitchell had been one of hopeful realism rather than an indication of U.S. emigration plans as a certainty. The diminishing prospect of American labor received its last mention in Governor Seymour's annual address to the colonial assembly on January 21, 1864, duly transmitted to Washington by Consul Leas. The governor expressed optimism for the eventual "revocation of the prohibition in regards to procuring "Contrabands" from the United States," though nothing further came of the issue.[37]

There were other options that could be exercised, moreover, toward which the British colonies in general had been moving for a while. In addition to the more-established East Indian laborers, or "coolies" as they were pejoratively called, the tropical possessions of the Empire were putting together the parts of a nascent system of Chinese immigration in the early 1860s, despite doubts about such workers' quality and reliability.[38] Indeed, the old Hyde, Hodge and Company had introduced Guiana's first such cargo in 1853, that colony being the trailblazer among the British territories in this respect. London entrusted Guiana with greater leeway over immigration, believing the colony to be less open to abuse than its other Caribbean holdings.[39]

The BHC's subsequent correspondence with the Colonial Office suggests that it soon reconciled itself to the thought of filling the New River Lagoon site with Chinese laborers, although the location is not named in its appeals for them; presumably this point either went without saying or was not considered an important part of their application to the British Emigration Board. As early as May 1864, the BHC and British Honduras' new governor,

John Gardiner Austin, were thrashing out the conditions under which the colonial secretary would permit such a labor importation; the sources contain references to certain houses and hospitals as being under construction, matching the earlier descriptions of Leas and the American visitors. Hodge placed an order for 300 Chinese immigrants in June 1864. Tellingly, this is the same number that he mentioned to Mitchell in October 1863, when he still held out some hope of obtaining black Americans. In April 1865, Hodge also paid the voyage for a Methodist clergyman to visit company land, apparently attempting to attract teachers for the settlers. His letter back to a British missionary society described a small but growing settlement near the New River with 131 emigrants having recently arrived from Barbados.[40]

Indeed, even before the bad news from London, the BHC had a crop to harvest and in September 1863 had checked with the Colonial Office if it was allowed to obtain Mexicans from the neighboring province of Yucatán.[41] Holding preferences for U.S. contrabands did not preclude the company from keeping other options open.

Hodge's more interesting reaction to the failure to obtain southern ex-slaves, though, was his attempt to obtain their former masters, though presumably offering them far greater personal freedom and better conditions. The faltering fortunes of the Confederacy on the battlefield displaced white southerners and slaves alike with many of the former turning to Central America to start anew. British Honduras's undeveloped lands and continuous pleas for farmers to cultivate them made the colony particularly appealing to fleeing southerners. Belize eventually became home to members of several prominent southern families, including those of Joseph Benjamin, the brother of Judah P. Benjamin, and Colin J. McRae, the former Confederate financial agent in Europe. They formed an expatriate community in the colony's northern agricultural region, appropriately dubbed "New Richmond."[42]

Consul Leas first reported the influx of Confederates in March 1864. The migrants informed him "the Confederacy is lost, that no hope can be longer entertained, and having lost their fortunes in the south . . . they have came to British Honduras to live and die."[43] Hodge received similar reports from the southerners, along with word that the North was "arming all the negroes." This affirmed Hodge's suspicions about the War Department's contrabands policy, prompting him to write London on March 24 that "they do not expect to obtain negro labour from thence until after the war ceases."[44] White southerners, on the other hand, could satisfy the company's need for cotton farmers.

In August 1864 Governor Austin reported the outcome of a conversation that had happened some time previously between Hodge, Leas, and himself in which Hodge had taken hope at the arrival in the colony of white men fleeing the Confederacy and had asked the consul to press the State Department to allow ships carrying such *émigrés* to depart the easily reached but Union-occupied New Orleans and to grant the colony of British Honduras a pass to break the blockade. Leas had indeed transmitted this on to Seward, being personally convinced that it was "politic and humane"—and presumably quietly open to the notion that depriving the Confederacy of manpower could only be a good thing—and reported back that the secretary of state "had the matter under consideration."[45]

More likely Seward shared the opinion of the Colonial Office: Hodge's hope that the southerners could become naturalized British subjects was quite out of the question. The situation was "obviously of the greatest delicacy" and one on which "it was perfectly impossible for him to expect any sort of opinion."[46] Such an exodus would occur after the war, buoyed in part by Hodge taking it upon himself to tour the South and peddle the idea, while some Confederates had, of course, already made their way to Belize. But given the diplomatic embarrassments which had surrounded the contraband issue even after January 1, 1863, for Hodge to have hoped for official sanction for the idea must count as one of his more fanciful moments.

Yet efforts to recruit African Americans in particular had indeed come to a halt for British Honduras. The issue was not dead, though, for at the same time that Hodge's mixed fortunes and the vacillating hand of government swung against him for the final time, interest in Guiana, where no such interdiction had been placed, was peaking.

Chapter 6

A Self-Supporting Scheme

A combination of Hodge's personal presence in Washington, D.C., and the simple timeliness of his approach made the British Honduras scheme the most developed of Lincoln's second wave of colonization projects, those in which the partnership of foreign governments would be sought as a surety against the pitfalls of the 1862 negotiations and the corruption of the Île à Vache contract. Its shadow, though a meager part of a historical literature that has tended to neglect all postemancipation colonization programs, could easily obscure other contemporary projects of a similar purpose. Two such efforts, one in British Guiana and a similar program in neighboring Dutch Surinam, replicated the familiar design of the Honduras policy wherein the United States attempted to negotiate an agreement with established European powers to designate specified northern port cities as points of emigration and, from each, induce a voluntary mass migration of the freedmen's population to the Caribbean. Guiana somewhat paralleled Hodge's negotiations, albeit with a different political strategy, while Surinam developed through the entirely independent channels of the State Department. Both bear discussion, as they illustrate a long-forgotten component of the colonization story as well as the comprehensive intent of its "emigration" phase, announced to Congress by Lincoln in December 1862.

From the perspective of the American records, Guiana takes something of a backseat compared to British Honduras in the negotiations with the Lincoln administration, with Dickson appearing to attach himself to Hodge's efforts in May or June 1863. But this is not entirely deserved. If anything, Guiana had paid attention to events in the U.S. too early, Walker's mission being more premature than ill-conceived. The colony continued to show interest after Hodge and the BHC started to look elsewhere for labor, culminating in an April 1864 proclamation of the three aforementioned ports per the 1863 agreement. Guiana reached this point under different circumstances from British Honduras, however.

Governor Hincks, like others in the colonial and diplomatic services, had his misgivings about the prospects of emigration. His opening letter on the matter to the Duke of Newcastle expressed doubts that America's black population could be checked by removal and wondered what the appeal of the colonies could be when America had so much uncultivated land in need of development. This was an especially pertinent question, since what Britain offered would involve free men having to tolerate being placed under minimum three-year indenture unless they could pay their passage.[1] His instructions to Walker stressed the need to downplay the significance of the indenture system: he was to dismiss it as purely about reimbursement of the share of passage paid by the planter, as well as to present it as beneficial to the laborer due to the body of protective laws that it entailed.[2] The pamphlet that Walker brought to distribute in the United States, *The Emigration of the Emancipated Negroes to British Guiana,* was written in such vein.

Not that Hincks was averse to schemes of freer migration, though, suggesting a government-backed system of internal "colonization" of Guiana's virtually empty frontier. In this model, settlers would receive title to the soil after a series of generously spaced repayments amounting to no more than the actual cost of house and land. It was only experimental, and he acknowledged that it did involve a massive initial hurdle of requiring settlers pay travel costs out of their own pockets. But he was enthusiastic, and it had clearly been a pet project of his for a while: "I had worked out the details of such a scheme for the benefit of the poor whites of Barbados [his previous posting] . . . the essence of such a scheme is that it should be self-supporting . . . in the peculiar circumstances of this Colony its advantage to the Creole population would be almost beyond conception."[3]

This was a more enlightened vision than the Guyanese planters were amenable to receiving. The colony's survival in the face of cheap slave-grown sugar—where other now-free producers of the foodstuff had struggled desperately to remain competitive—was founded on the maintenance of a plantation labor force short of slavery but enforced by strict discipline, limitations on the size of Creole settlements (to bring hands back to the plantation), and an even harsher indenture system from 1854.[4] By this point the old absentee landlords had mostly gone to the wall and been replaced by more efficient capitalist managers of the plantations, whose actual presence in the colony offered sizable scope for manipulation of the government, and more rapid responses to emerging opportunities, than in the past.

British Honduras and Guiana present some superficial similarities in this period. Both were controlled by a small group of powerful elites, and both were trying to obtain American labor and to adjust the rules on landholding, immigration, and credit limits at the London banks in their favor. But Hincks also felt such pressure to a greater extent, as Guiana was a plantation society while Belize was not. Indeed the latter was attempting a more novel, tentative transformation in its agricultural basis, whereas the former was trying to shore up its dominant, long-established sugar industry along predictable lines. On the other hand, though, there was not in Guiana a monopolistic company like the BHC seeking immigrants for specific projects, so this left the nature of any influx more open-ended and contestable. This last point was especially true as Hincks was determined to calm the ethnic and class tensions engendered by earlier, less regulated waves of labor importation.

In the swirl of competing ideas, Dickson's plans were closer to the idealistic end of the spectrum (albeit not without some deference to the colony's needs, or devoid of the use of indenture), but it is hard to see what importance he really held in the absence of evidence about the nature of the emigration from the U.S. that he hoped to foment. Whereas Hodge had taken an expedition to British Honduras in an attempt to publicize the venture to influential African Americans, a high-risk strategy, Dickson's approach was far more low-key and provided Guiana with an agent constantly present in the U.S. who offered a less erratic approach to its interests. He was no mercenary publicist, having visited the colony at some point in early 1862 to "project a gas company," and from 1863 sought several updates from Lyons as to the state of the question. When the contraband obstruction was lifted, he apparently entered into correspondence with unnamed parties as to the disposition to settle in Guiana.

Dickson also wrote to Hincks to suggest the formation of an unincorporated company with the power to hold land, based on the model black community founded by the Elgin Association in Ontario, with the kind of village settlement that would move away from the plantation system and its concomitant scourge of landless and incentive-deprived laborers, while still allowing for indentures to grow the cotton for which the world was proving so hungry during the war.[5] This might have chimed with Hincks's internal colonization model as expressed to Newcastle, and although he did not explicitly make the comparison, the governor did forward Dickson's idea to London for consideration. It was too abstract for practical policymaking, though: the Colonial Office responded that "it is unnecessary to discuss the merits for a hypothetical scheme of which the outline and objects are very vaguely explained."[6]

Indeed, idealism was not the order of the day. Planter excitement reached fever pitch when news from the United States arrived in the colony, not only of the June 1863 agreement, but of the lifting of the Foreign Office's objections to contrabands, too. Hincks issued Ordinance No. 14 in 1863 to allow the introduction of laborers from the United States and the other British colonies, in contravention of the normal Colonial Office ban on what it saw as the economically irrational practice of imperial possessions recruiting from one another. Barbados—home to a large landless population—had provided fertile ground for Antiguan recruiters, a fact of which the planters had become aware. The ordinance simply extended the existing Indian and Chinese legislation to these potential emigrants with the exception of keeping the length of indenture at three years rather than the five which London permitted from 1862. This was possibly intended as an incentive to would-be laborers who came from parts of the world where they might expect more privileged arrangements than those granted to less "civilized" groups.

Reporting on a public meeting which had formed itself in Georgetown (the capital) at the news, and which contained many key merchants and the mayor, Hincks felt that their original aim was to acquire Barbadians first and Americans if necessary, but that their plans were already tending inexorably toward the latter. He told Newcastle that he was under pressure to show the full Foreign Office correspondence on the contrabands question, the confidential parts included. He also reported that the more enthusiastic were already planning massive loans from Britain so that the entire cost of their importation could be covered up front and then placed fully on the colonial treasury through taxation on the lame pretext that the existing compromise of the government paying one-third and the planters two-thirds—which had itself been seen as a regrettable concession to the estate capitalists—applied only to the Indians and Chinese. Suspecting that shipping interests were involved and seeing this as a way to run profitable lines between the U.S. and Guiana, Hincks urged rejection.[7]

The governor was under massive pressure from a restive planting element though. The Colonial Office concurred with his objections to the changes proposed by the Georgetown meeting, but as one London official noted, his quick shift in position to recommending a Guyanese bounty incentive in the U.S. excited suspicion that he was coming round to the estate managers' point of view too easily.[8] The *Times* also pointed the finger at their lobbying, reporting that the Court of Policy had hesitated on the issue—as the introduction of labor tended to pit the interests of the employers against those of the employed—but that a signed address from pro-immigration elements had likely swayed the governor. The newspaper urged care in the matter with respect to relations with the Confederacy, conceding that individual emigrants were "entitled to our protection on British territory," while arguing that an official system was a different matter and far more likely to embroil London in difficulties. Equally if not more true to form, it sneered that most emigrant workers would be unskilled and of an inferior quality not worth importing and that the "clever Yankee" would use the bait of a passage to Guiana to rescue runaways who had not joined the army from the "misery" that they currently endured.[9]

In any case, the matter became of critical importance when the Colonial Office decided to put a stop to Barbadian emigration at the request of that island's governor, thus depriving the Guyanese planters of their first choice for recruitment. Hincks felt that he had just one option left, one that was far more to do with satisfying the elite than any real expectation of emigration.[10] Under the power vested in him by Ordinance No. 4 of 1864, on April 6, 1864, he proclaimed the ports of Boston, New York, and Philadelphia for emigration to Guiana at $25 bounty per head. Willet Rowe of New York was designated official agent for conveying settlers.[11] Certifying all this was a familiar face, Government Secretary Walker, who had himself stepped into the role of effective governor of the colony on four occasions in its turbulent political past.

Having previously doubted the sincerity of pro-immigration feelings, when he had entertained suspicions that mercantile and shipping interests had been the real puppeteers at the Georgetown meeting (interested in an excessive London loan and emigrant contracts, respectively), Hincks conceded that he had had 2,000 *bona fide* labor applications from plantations for a limit of 500 immigrant places. There were other hints of sugar growers' desperation, the governor's reduction of the contractual term to one year suggesting that he was trying to fill immediate vacancies on whatever terms, rather than setting in motion an exodus of long-term manpower for the colony. He had no faith in the scheme, a sentiment with which the Colonial Office agreed, finding it impossible to see how Guiana could appeal to African Americans while it offered less than one-fourth the wage rate to which they were accustomed.[12]

By this point, indeed, it was almost a completely hypothetical affair. As with British Honduras, no mass immigration of freedmen ever materialized, but Her Majesty's Government put a surprising amount of thought into how it would deal with the matter should it ever come about. An immediate April 1864 concern was that emigration agents for the colonies should be under consular authority and use that medium for contact with the U.S. government, as had been projected during 1862–1863, whereas a July 1864 communication apparently had Russell and the new colonial secretary Edward Cardwell agreed on keeping the matter *away* from the British consuls or any officer of the home government—presumably a contrary slant on the same underlying hope of keeping the matter free of diplomatic upset—and in the hands of colonial agents instead.[13] But "accounts from the United States appear to show that nothing short of compulsion will induce the coloured population to emigrate"; compulsion was not going to be used; and, therefore, only a speculative opinion could be formed on a hypothetical point.[14]

One curious voice of objection was that of Edward Archibald, British consul at New York. He told the government of his fears that colonial subagents would be necessarily partial and resort to kidnapping, a problem that London hoped to avoid by using someone settled in the prospective port of departure, who would therefore be more answerable for the employment of questionable methods than a transient colonial would be.[15] Indeed Archibald, who ended up in Britain in mid-1864, met Russell to convince him of the need to be very careful about the use of a bounty system as proclaimed by Guiana, and of the burden that consuls might face if forced to assist in ship inspections and at the point of embarkation. On this count he persuaded the foreign secretary, which might alone explain Russell's *volte-face* on the place of Her Majesty's consuls in the process.[16]

Guiana's offer of bounties remains slightly intriguing, as it had recent, firsthand experience with the complications that they brought. Hincks reported in late 1863 that agents from Dutch Surinam were using them to poach Guiana's laborers and added that he well understood why Barbados had stopped bounty recruitment on its soil, as the temptation tended to prove too great for laborers to think carefully before they signed up. Hincks did however reckon that such rewards had a place in recruitment for Guiana in the U.S., as long as there was proper consular inspection of the emigrant ships. This was taken by the Colonial Office as a hint of the planters' supposed influence over him, as noted.[17]

Archibald's motives in remonstrating against Guiana's move are otherwise somewhat unclear. He was undoubtedly aware of the BHC's work with Garnet and their efforts to secure a ship the previous fall. If the new project went ahead, New York would again become the primary port of embarkation for emigrants, and he had seen how explosive an African American presence could be during the draft riots, when he had been forced to offer sanctuary to hounded black sailors from British West Indian vessels and even to telegraph Lyons to get a warship placed on standby.[18] Archibald had also been a witness to earlier colonization efforts, asked by Lyons to investigate the background of the Île à Vache project since that had originated on his turf, too.[19] But it would have taken being present on that island, and not at the American end of the project, to associate colonization with manifest neglect. Indeed it is almost more through the abstract categorization of the historian that one treats the two projects together, and Archibald surely cannot have feared that his own country would act as shamefully as individual investors had, especially with all the protections that the American and British governments had negotiated.

There is one very interesting link between Archibald and colonization, though. He was a close associate of Ambrose W. Thompson, the head of the Chiriqui Improvement Company, and seems to have enjoyed a very warm relationship with him. Mixing personal and patriotic interests in a way which perhaps did not seem quite so questionable in the nineteenth century, he most likely had a stake in the company, had certainly asked Thompson for help with a loan, and had written him a letter of introduction to Lord Lyons in 1860. Yet Archibald had less corrupt reasons to show interest in Thompson's transisthmian holdings, too. In early 1861, when Congress had had Chiriquí under consideration as a coaling station and harbor (before its revival during the Civil War as a site for colonization), he had found himself preaching to the choir when trying to convince Lyons of its potential value in reducing the distance between parts of the British Empire. Though he kept quiet about his involvement on that occasion, by 1865 he took advantage of Thompson's attempts to float a new Chiriquí company in Britain by openly applying to the Foreign Office for permission to join the board of directors to represent the interests of London.[20]

Since the administration's Chiriquí scheme was technically only ever suspended, it might have been that he was privately hoping to sabotage Guiana's bid, lest it drain the well of potential emigrants for a project that he preferred and which might yet go ahead. But without any evidence of such thinking on his part, or indeed any hint in the sources as to the prospects for Chiriquí's revival, this has to remain an aside. It would not be unreasonable to conjecture that as the New York consul, Archibald was the most in danger of facing an extra burden if emigration commenced and that his reasoning went no further than that.

Guiana's proclamation does not seem to have been countermanded, but the British government remained cautious, and might have intervened more forcefully in checking recruitment if the colony had actually been able to find potential settlers in the U.S. Whitehall asked Lyons for a general report on the question in August 1864, and he replied only in February 1865 due to a prolonged absence. He asserted that Washington should be consulted again on the matter (even though there had been no official change in the administration's stance) and that any agents should be neither private speculators, nor from the British consulates and legation—but that they should take instructions from the latter. This was necessary "to prevent complicated questions with the United States authorities," hinting at the legation's frustrations with the War Department during the previous year's canvassing efforts. His law officer at the legation qualified this by pointing out that government policy was nominally still that of colonization, that there were no laws against voluntary black emigration, and yet agreed that the Guiana scheme was still dangerous.[21]

The exact nature of these fears is hard to discern but was apparently not about contrabands in particular—although given the uncertain outcome of the war right up until late 1864, it would be no surprise if this still weighed heavily on British minds—so much as diplomatic embarrassments from more general abuses. After the war, such objections seem to have been eventually lifted—although there was an unwillingness to pursue the matter even into 1865 and 1866, with renewed permission only granted to Honduras in July of that year—but it was too late, and the issue seems to have been one of low priority and even indifference on the part of the government.[22]

Paradoxically, the war that had breathed more life than ever into the possibility of colonization also beset it with complications that induced a deep conservatism and caution in imperial officials who in principle craved labor. The narrowing of the scope for diplomatic entanglement and the newfound peace of mind in London with respect to emigration were due to the termination of the war, yet the very same occurrence also set in train events which would convince the few African Americans who still needed to be persuaded that their future lay in the United States and not elsewhere.

A rare photograph of Lord Lyons and Henry Pelham-Clinton, fifth Duke of Newcastle and secretary of state for the colonies. Newcastle oversaw the development of emigration proposals from British Honduras and Guiana, whereas Lyons coordinated the negotiations with Washington. The two are shown here accompanying Albert Edward, the Prince of Wales and later King Edward VII, during a visit to the United States. The photograph was taken in Portland, Maine, on October 20, 1860. (Library of Congress)

Richard Bickerton Pemell Lyons, first Viscount Lyons. While serving as British minister to Washington during the Lincoln administration, Lyons was authorized to oversee all negotiations concerning the relocation of black emigrants to the British West Indies. Photograph by Matthew Brady, circa 1860-1865. (Library of Congress)

Frederick Seymour, lieutenant governor of British Honduras from 1862 to 1864. In September 1863 Seymour authorized the proclamation of three U.S. ports as points of emigration for the recruitment of black laborers. He is pictured here while serving as the governor of British Columbia. Photograph by Frederick Dally, circa 1866. (Royal British Columbia Museum, BC Archives)

Sir Francis Hincks, governor of British Guiana from 1862 to 1869. As governor, Hincks oversaw the Walker mission to the United States of 1862 and authorized the recruitment of black laborers from the United States in 1864. Hincks had a long and distinguished career in Canadian politics, and is pictured here late in life as a member of the Canadian parliament. (McCord Museum MP–1991.12.6)

The Rev. James Mitchell of Indiana was appointed emigration commissioner by Lincoln in 1862 to oversee the implementation of colonization. Mitchell was the Lincoln administration's leading advocate of immigration to British Honduras and Guiana. He later became entangled in a budgetary dispute with John P. Usher that contributed to the repeal of the colonization budget in 1864. This photograph was taken around 1880 when Mitchell was the headmaster of the Mt. Zion Seminary in Carroll County, Georgia. (Image courtesy of Jack Dorsey, Mt. Zion Community Center, Mt. Zion, Georgia)

J. Willis Menard was a well-known African American proponent of colonization and was hired on as a clerk in the Emigration Office, becoming the first African American to hold an administrative position within the United States government. In 1868 Menard became the first African American to win election to the United States Congress, but he was eventually refused his seat in favor of a white candidate who challenged the election results. He was permitted to make a speech before Congress on February 23, 1869. (Library of Congress)

Major-General Benjamin F. Butler met in private with President Lincoln at the White House on April 11, 1865, three days before the assassination. According to Butler, Lincoln discussed with him the possibility of reviving colonization after the Civil War by recruiting black laborers to dig the Panama Canal. (Library of Congress)

John Palmer Usher, secretary of the interior from 1863 to 1865. Known as a generally unassuming administrator to most, Usher nonetheless became entangled in a prolonged feud over the colonization fund that contributed more than any other factor to the British project's collapse. Usher likely knew Mitchell from their prior careers in Indiana politics, suggesting that the source of the feud may have predated the Lincoln administration. (Library of Congress)

Rev. Henry Highland Garnet (to upper left of Frederick Douglass) as he appeared in 1865. Garnet was the pastor of the Shiloh Presbyterian Church in New York City and an influential supporter of African repatriation within the black community. In 1863 he assisted the British Honduras Company's efforts to recruit colonists among the free black population of the north. (Library of Congress)

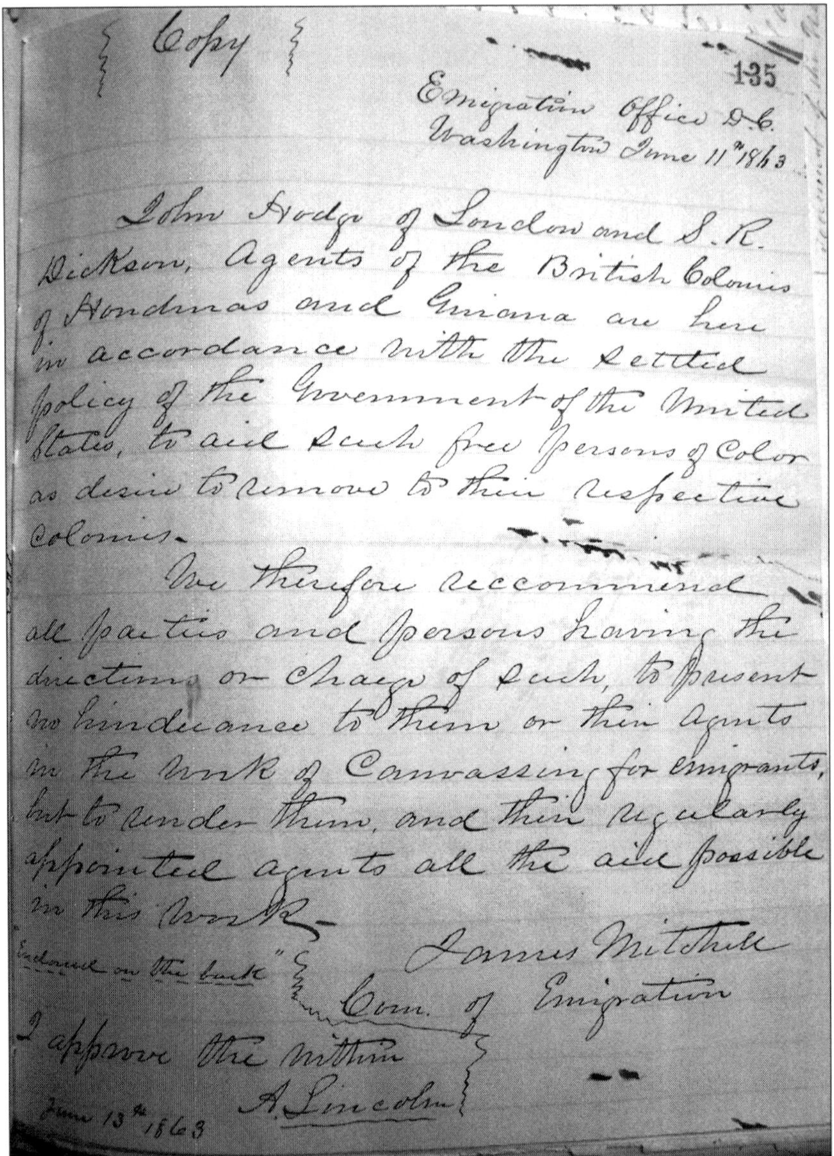
Copy

135

Emigration Office D.C.
Washington June 11th 1863

John Hodge of London and S. R. Dickson, Agents of the British Colonies of Honduras and Guiana are here in accordance with the settled policy of the Government of the United States, to aid such free persons of Color as desire to remove to their respective Colonies.

We therefore recommend all parties and persons having the direction or charge of such, to present no hindrance to them or their Agents in the work of Canvassing for emigrants, but to render them, and their regularly appointed agents all the aid possible in this work.

James Mitchell
Com. of Emigration

"Endorsed on the back"

I approve the within
A. Lincoln
June 13th 1863

The British Legation record of Abraham Lincoln's authorization to the emigration canvassers from British Honduras and Guiana. This first-generation copy is the best-preserved of three known surviving versions. (UK National Archives)

Chapter 7

Secretary Seward and the Dutch Treaty

If historians have tended to underestimate the complexity of Lincoln's abstract beliefs on colonization, there has been a danger, too, of oversimplifying the more down-to-earth questions of preference and timing which surround the emigration projects. In the conventional narrative, Chiriquí comes across as rejected outright, then superseded by the signing of the Île à Vache contract, and that shortly before colonization falls into oblivion—whether consciously allowed by politicians or otherwise. In fact, the administration never formally abandoned the Chiriquí project but rather put it on ice for what it could not have been sure would be an indefinite term, while the president was still negotiating with the British even as the Île à Vache settlers put to sea. This was the natural extension and stated intent of Lincoln's offer to "the several States situated within the Tropics" after regional opposition complicated the Chiriquí contract in late 1862. Given the ever-practical Lincoln's willingness to experiment, it should come as no surprise that he had several pots on the boil at once.

One astonishingly overlooked part of Civil War colonization history is the negotiations that the State Department undertook with the Netherlands for the better part of 1863, as another European empire responded positively to Seward's September 30, 1862, circular. The Dutch effort ran concurrent with the British schemes and, if anything, makes for an easier project to follow, limited strictly to State Department channels but leaving not even a ghost in the relevant Interior Department records. As such it escaped the associated baggage of interdepartment political maneuvering that constantly imperiled the projects in British Honduras and neighboring Guiana. Robert F. Durden accorded the Dutch effort generous coverage in his study of the U.S. wartime minister to The Hague (and longtime *New-York Tribune* columnist), James Shepherd Pike. As long ago as 1957, he rightly identified that "[t]his was much later than the foreign negotiations are generally believed to have lasted, and the project reached a surprisingly advanced stage."[1]

As with the plans for British Honduras and Guiana, the Dutch negotiations effectively died by early 1864 without concrete results and are actually harder to "read" than the others for insights into internal politics behind them. They left little beyond what exists in accompanying diplomatic records, since they apparently involved no more than normal, backroom ministerial negotiations, not involving a Hodge-like figure reporting from Washington or otherwise shedding light on Lincoln's personal stance and actions.[2] Nevertheless, the Dutch proposition was quite analogous to the president's intentions for the British tropical possessions—the colony in question was Dutch Guiana, or Surinam—and its significance really lies in the very fact of its happening, complementing as it does the authors' main focus on British Guiana and Honduras.

The Netherlands minister to the United States, Roest Van Limburg, had in fact asked Seward as early as July 1862 if the administration would consider an emigration scheme, suggesting a term of five years for laborers and indicating that it was The Hague which had directed him to look into the matter.[3] The secretary of state, true to form, expressed doubts over the prospects of success, since "it [was] believed the demand for laborers in that class in the military and naval service of the United States alone is sufficient to outweigh any inducement to their emigration abroad likely to be offered." He added, however, that the Dutch government could submit an application to the Department of the Interior if it wished to proceed.[4]

Unsurprisingly, The Hague was therefore delighted at Seward's more formal suggestion in the September circular, but negotiations would not get under way in earnest until mid-1863, at which point the Dutch foreign minister admitted to Pike that the matter "would not have remained so long unanswered if the Government of the King had been able to make that reply definitive, which it was impossible to do before the arrangements relative to the emigration of free laborers to Surinam could be determined."[5] Specifically, the Netherlands had, much like the British colonies, felt it necessary to pass new legislation to better meet the requirements of an influx of American contrabands, with William III decreeing two tailor-made ordinances in March 1863. This delay might account for why scholars looking for a more immediate response in the diplomatic dispatches have concluded that early Dutch interest went nowhere.

The first ordinance, "concerning the Control on the Introduction of Free Labourers into Surinam," restricted the ports of embarkation to those explicitly proclaimed, laid out standards for the conditions of the points of departure and the ships, and set an indenture of six days of eight hours per week, though it did not specify the overall term or wages. The second one, "concerning the Offer of Premiums by the Government on the Introduction of Free Labourers into Surinam," set the level of rewards for agents who organized emigration expeditions at forty guilders (about sixteen dollars) per male; men were to be sixteen to forty years of age.

This was significantly less generous than the rate offered per Chinese or Indian emigrant, and Durden posited that "[t]he Dutch apparently expected the Lincoln government's emancipation and colonization policies to flood the market with easily obtained Negro labor," hence the lower bounty. It is worth adding, though, that the ordinance split emigrants into two categories, those coming from west of the Cape of Good Hope and those coming from east of it, and while the latter did indeed incur the highest premium—perhaps on the grounds of the distance involved in transporting them—the African Americans would actually generate the highest premium per worker for the western zone. These ordinances were printed in English-language pamphlets, probably intended for distribution in the U.S. when the emigration treaty was ratified.[6]

The one American condition that The Hague contested was that of having to appoint itself an official agent for each expedition, the Dutch suggesting instead that they would rather provide for the work of supervision by simply making sure that those organizing the voyages were known to be of good reputation. This would bring the convention into line with the existing Dutch laws on the subject. The Hague also rejected Seward's earlier stipulation that an American citizen accompany the voyage. This presented no problem: the secretary of state declared the ordinances "liberal, just and precise" and in July 1863 granted Pike plenipotentiary status on the draft treaty that he sent as an enclosure. This qualified his circular by incorporating some of the provisions of the Dutch legislation, though Seward stressed that it would be amenable to both governments, "supplementary to, rather than conflicting with" his earlier demands, and he declared the convention "one as would probably be approved by the Senate and ratified by the President."[7]

Pike hammered out further adjustments with The Hague, reporting to Seward in October that the only change that the foreign minister had requested so far was one to the sixth article of the draft convention. This had stated rather ambiguously that emigrants would either receive land to cultivate on their own account or wages from working for others, to which the cabinet wished to add "according to agreement made between them and the engaging persons as defined by contract." The U.S. minister readily assented.[8]

The draft's use of the word *citizen* also raised Dutch eyebrows, Pike conceding to the foreign minister that the term could "hardly be deemed an accurate description of the subjects of a Prince" and acknowledging the "republican inadvertence" in the phraseology. He explained that the word's purpose had simply been to clarify that the settlers would receive the same rights as the other inhabitants of the colony and that he had felt that the Dutch choice of "resident" failed to distinguish between the native or naturalized populace and foreigners who did not enjoy the same privileges. But realizing that The Hague was not seeking to deny the emigrants the legal standing that the U.S. desired for them, Pike settled on the compromise of comparing them to "native residents."[9] Thereafter, it went to the king, and Pike reported on December 16 that the signing would happen that day and that the treaty would be sent by the next mail.[10]

The final version of the convention stated that the Dutch government or the governor of Surinam could authorize agents to recruit in the United States, such permission to be shown to the American authorities upon demand. The agent would have to compile thorough lists proving that the emigrants had given their free consent and provide "healthful and convenient accommodations" on board, with the settlers to be given "comfortable dwellings" once landed, and to be granted "all civil rights held by native residents in the colony."[11] The treaty incorporated the two changes mentioned above and a merely semantic adjustment in the wording of another article but was otherwise the same as what Seward had sent to Pike.[12]

The minister himself was not an enthusiast for any of this. Confusingly, Pike had in fact long held personal proclivities for the separation of the white and black races. He had called for the setting aside of the Caribbean for black expatriation as early as 1853, before there was even a Republican party, let alone its Central American colonizationist element.[13] More recently, he had told his political intimate Senator William P. Fessenden that he held out hopes for the formation of a "Negro pen" within the boundaries of the U.S.[14] For whatever reason, though, he disliked the Dutch scheme. In April 1864, he asked Fessenden to refuse to ratify the treaty if it came the Senate's way, "[n]ot that I believe it would do any harm in its operation, but because I think the principle on which it is based, a vicious one."[15] As Durden argued, it is quite hard to fathom what a racial separatist's objections to it would have been in principle. There is a chance that Pike had come round by this date to a preference for domestic colonization (that is to say, within the U.S. but in an outlying area) over foreign, a distinction which seems disingenuous to the modern reader but one to which some contemporaries sincerely subscribed, as they tried to reconcile their pessimistic sentiments on race with concerns such as a reluctance to pay extra taxes for colonization, skepticism over the feasibility of foreign expatriation, and a desire to use internal resettlement to remold and punish the South.[16] Alternatively, Pike's reservations might have had something to do with what he knew of Dutch intent—but if so, he did not elaborate.

In any event, he need not have warned Fessenden. The treaty was never submitted to the Senate, Seward telling Pike in what is hard not to read as a postscript for the administration's proactive pursuit of colonization. "I am obliged to confess that it is not now expected that the treaty in regard to negro emigration will be ratified. The American people have advanced to a new position in regard to slavery and the African class since the President in obedience to their prevailing wishes accepted the policy of colonization. Now not only their free labor, but their military service also is appreciated and accepted."[17]

The secretary of state broke the news to the Dutch around the same time. Van Limburg had asked Seward days earlier what ports of embarkation the U.S. would allow the Netherlands to proclaim to which the secretary of state promptly replied along similar lines—that the Senate had not yet ratified the treaty but that in any case "it was doubtful whether it will be confirmed by that body in view of the altered condition of affairs relating to the treaty since the negotiation commenced."[18]

The last word on the matter came in a March 1864 dispatch from Pike acknowledging Seward's report. "This government receives with regret the intimation that the Treaty . . . is not likely to be ratified," he reported, adding that the Colonial Department had been particularly keen to take the credit for obtaining labor for a colony which desperately desired it. He could not resist adding his own opinion, though, as to "the good policy on our part of rejecting [it]."[19]

The Dutch public had known about the negotiations and signing at The Hague, the planters of Surinam hastily chasing up the U.S. consul in the capital, Paramaribo, at the news, but thereafter the convention seems to have quietly slipped from the records.[20] This would make sense, since rejection occurred behind closed doors and was conveyed to the Netherlands in a slightly open-ended and less than definitive manner. (It is not in the general nature of things, moreover, to make an announcement in respect to something that has fizzled out.) In May 1864, the New York firm of L. Marx and Company, possibly fishing for a contract, wrote to the State Department reporting that its Dutch contacts had picked up on the treaty and were wondering if it had been ratified (and if not, the reasons for rejection).[21] On the other hand, the firm might have known that the convention was abortive and been more interested in the explanation. The authors have not, however, attempted to trace the affair within the Dutch sources.

Drawing inferences from the diplomatic records on the project, other than the obvious ones, is difficult, and Lincoln's own writings yield no overt references. Certainly it seems highly improbable that Seward was negotiating the treaty with anything other than Lincoln's full knowledge, especially given his personal dislike of colonization. It is not credible, either, that he scuppered it without the same, his reluctance on the British project and other points of disagreement with Lincoln having never translated into anything more overtly disobedient than foot-dragging. His explanation to Pike, framing both colonization's earlier endorsement and its current obsolescence in terms of the president's deference to public opinion, chimes with what some recent scholars have tried to argue. But in light of the broad content of this study, this was obviously quite one-sided, and reads more like a loyal attempt to avoid tarring Lincoln with the brush of failure while still signaling that colonization was going nowhere.

Seward's statement that black emigration had become too unpopular to pass the Senate was on the mark, but even if the insight was President Lincoln's, it offers nothing either way on the president's private beliefs or putative willingness to continue pursuing colonization had other means presented themselves. This was just after the British plans had also hit a wall, after all, and it marks the beginning of the period when the sources begin to get very patchy and fragmentary other than for the winding-up of Île à Vache. More striking, perhaps, is that up until this point Lincoln might have been trying to keep up the negotiations for the formal convention that had eluded him in Britain's case. This would indicate a continued preference to place colonization on a sounder, more regulated footing than that offered by Latin American opposition and shady businessmen's private concessions.

Of course, per Lincoln's other projects, the emigration was to be strictly voluntary. Seward was perhaps hinting at his personal doubts over the effectiveness of a scheme free of coercion when he told Pike that those "who have become free by the operations of the war, are earning a livelihood by their own exertions" and that they were "at liberty to make their own bargains and to take charge of their own interests with a view to emigration abroad."[22] In this sense, the secretary might have felt comfortable indulging Lincoln by doing his bidding, knowing that the idea was unfeasible.

Durden offered the speculation, too—albeit wisely withholding judgment on the matter for his own part—that Seward had a diplomatic trick up his sleeve, one of tying the Dutch materially to Union interests, much as the British suspected in the case of their own negotiations.[23] Of note in this respect is the Union's success in selling bonds on the German and Dutch markets around this time, while British capitalists had proved more unwilling.[24] This was a promising development that Seward might have wanted to consolidate further, not least since the Confederacy had not been entirely unsuccessful either in European banking circles, with its March 1863 coup of the Erlanger loan.

But this all seems too evasive and cast somewhat in the mold of the colonization literature's tendency to see contrived ruses and overelaborate political appeals where the facts of the matter would be better taken at face value. Both of the above considerations applied equally to the British project, on which Seward tried to report unfavorably. Indeed, no point had been more crucial for trying to forestall European pro-southern dalliances than September 1862, when he had revealed the administration's hand to the British *chargé* with his shockingly frank admission of his differences with the president over colonization and of his doubts that anything would come of attempts to colonize.

One has to wonder as well what Seward made, if anything, of the would-be destination of the settlers. When the Dutch Legation first approached the administration, Surinam had not yet even abolished slavery, though admittedly Pike had informed Seward as early as June 1862 that emancipation had been under consideration for a long time and was imminent, being set for July 1, 1863, due to the emergence of a liberal government in the Netherlands.[25]

This occurred as planned, the cannons of Fort Zeelandia in Paramaribo proclaiming the act just hours before gunfire would start to ring out thousands of miles away at Gettysburg. Freedom had actually been in the works ever since the shock of sudden French and Danish West Indian emancipation in 1848 and had been held back by what was essentially the lack of an abolitionist lobby in the Netherlands and by fears of the scale of compensation required for the 33,000 slaves in Dutch Guiana and several thousand others in the outlying Dutch Antilles. With commissioners put in place to inform the slaves of what was coming, and the armed presence in the colony increased, the transition went relatively smoothly. The

American emigrants, moreover, would have all their guarantees as laid down in the treaty.

Yet the fact remains that Seward, and presumably Lincoln, had entered into negotiations for resettlement in a colony about to undergo the inherently unpredictable transition from bondage to free labor. Historians have noted that there was indeed an undercurrent of tension in Surinam in summer 1863 caused by the prospect of decade-long apprenticeships and imminent compulsory contracts for the freedmen.[26] The dispatches from the Paramaribo consulate, which enthusiastically stressed the need for African American labor, and the bargaining power that ex-slaves would enjoy, quite unwittingly hinted—in so doing—at the drawbacks of the colony. The settlers' scope for success was linked inextricably to the general stagnation and misery which had been caused by the manpower shortage, suggested consul Henry Sawyer, so brightly and unironically as to make one suspect that he had some kind of vested interest in the plantations. Surinam was in a "deplorable" condition, and trade was at a standstill; the planters were suffering as the slaves behaved shiftlessly in anticipation of freedom, and yet the latter's outlook was dreary too, faced with the prospect of qualified liberty.[27] While this all testified to the economic potential that industrious contrabands might enjoy, it was not a ringing endorsement of the general atmosphere which would permeate their new life.

As secretary of state, Seward would have had the best access of anyone to this information, information that could have fostered the misgivings that we know he was already harboring. It seems unlikely that there is much evidence out there on the minutiae of the drafting of the project, and even the timing of its whimpering demise is elusive. Pike did not hear from Seward on the matter between July 1863 and early the next year, when he declared it dead in the water. Due to such irregular correspondence, we cannot be sure of the exact point at which Lincoln jettisoned the convention. In fairness, one might have expected Seward to report this quickly, and perhaps with a touch of enthusiasm, had the president given the order sooner. Indeed, to assert even that much assumes that Lincoln made a discrete command, rather than that the secretary of state realized that he could quietly write its obituary in the face of silence over colonization from his boss and changed circumstances. One would assume that this was unlikely to be the case, but the dry sources of State Department and ministerial dispatches yield so very little in terms of motivation.

For these reasons, Pike's instructions and negotiations are best treated as a counterpart and not the equivalent, interpretatively, of the British Guiana and Honduras plans. Yet while difficult to fully comprehend in themselves, one thing that is worth remembering is the force of Seward's recollections of his differences with Lincoln over colonization. That this issue was prominently on his mind as he lay bedridden in the wake of something as distracting as an assassination attempt is striking.[28]

Perhaps it testifies not only to his objections in principle to colonization, but also to the fact that, in the face of emerging political divisions over colonization at the Interior Department, his State Department had been unwillingly charged with an elevated role in the case of the British projects and an exclusive one in the yet-more-questionable Netherlands option. Their effective failure, moreover, had come barely more than a year before Lincoln's death, and if the president had thereafter been open to renewing colonization, and Seward knew this, then he also would have understood that these possibilities might yet be revived.

Chapter 8

Administrative Dysfunction, Congressional Displeasure

James Mitchell's unexpectedly deft political maneuvering in May and June 1863 almost single-handedly reversed the fortunes of the Honduras and Guiana colonization projects. With the British principals disposed to abandon their quest for labor to politics, the lowly emigration commissioner outflanked two hostile members of the cabinet, secured the blessings of a third, and delivered an order from the president's desk giving sanction to the recruitment of black colonists from the United States. By the end of 1863 all signs suggested emigration would soon be under way. Furthermore, for the time being colonization remained the official policy of the Lincoln administration.

President Lincoln established the Emigration Office in 1862 to administer the government's colonization projects. Mitchell's post entitled him to a salary equivalent to that of a "chief clerk" of the Interior Department at $1,800 annually. This compensation, along with his budget, came directly from the colonization fund, and his appointment existed at the president's discretion.[1] Mitchell operated his office according to this arrangement without incident at the Interior Department under Caleb Smith, seeking the secretary's guidance in the formative stages of the colonization program. Mitchell initially favored funding emigration to Liberia through the established network of the American Colonization Society, though Smith urged him to wait for "other arrangements" being contemplated by the State Department, "which have not been consummated." With the secretary's approval, he assembled a staff of two assistant clerks, including Augustus A. Smith and Menard, the latter being the first African American ever hired for an administrative position in a federal agency. They were housed in a single room of the government's Pension Office Building, furnished by the colonization fund.[2]

The British Honduras project is a testament to Mitchell's occasional political acumen, seldom acknowledged by historical opinion. He is typically known for "provoking the ire of the successive secretaries of the Interior," which "only weakened" the administration's colonization efforts, to quote Gabor Boritt. In actuality, Mitchell enjoyed the favor of his first superior, Smith, and was personally friendly with several other members of the cabinet, including Blair and Attorney General Bates. [3] His quarrelsome reputation stems entirely from a single prolonged dispute with Smith's successor, John Palmer Usher, catalyzed by the events of May and June 1863.[4]

The circumvention of Stanton and Usher showed Mitchell's political talent at its finest. This ability inconsistently manifested itself. Even Mitchell's letters meander from astute and focused insights, replete with eminently practical strategies to advance a specific policy, to the interminable harangues of a revivalist preacher who quite literally approached colonization as if it were the nation's prophetic destiny. Mitchell's personality encompassed numerous irritating traits. Opinionated, prying, quick to speak his mind, and desirous of immediate results, he had little patience for Washington's bureaucratic hierarchy and procedure. Knowing these cavalier tendencies and habit of interspersing sermons with his policy writings, Lyons and Hodge often took great care to validate Mitchell's proclamations with the cabinet before acting on his word alone.[5]

The summer 1863 victory proved a temporary one for the same reasons that enabled its successes. When Mitchell outmaneuvered his immediate superior on colonization he unwittingly instigated a feud that outlived Lincoln and spilled into the Andrew Johnson administration. The War Department was none too pleased to learn that Lincoln applied his pen to the order Mitchell drafted with Hodge and Dickson. Usher concurred. The meddlesome emigration commissioner needed to go.

Usher had few options to rein in the cause of his annoyance directly. Mitchell's salary came from an earmarked account, and a direct presidential appointment prevented his dismissal without Lincoln's approval. The secretary's position still gave him influence over colonization policy, and any expenditure from the colonization account required his stamp. On May 18, as Mitchell conferred with Hodge, Usher decided to test the president's receptivity to eliminating the Emigration Office. Citing the "recent action of the War Department," budgetary constraints, and a need for additional room in the Pension Office, he requested "that the further attention of Revd. Mr. Mitchell . . . be dispensed with."[6] Lincoln patiently ignored the secretary's carefully worded request; he intended for Mitchell's office to administer the impending projects with Hodge and Dickson.

The summer of 1863 passed in relative peace as Mitchell continued work on the British arrangements, albeit in an uncooperative department. Usher strictly controlled the colonization fund and imposed the self-contradictory policy of limiting it to proposals involving the blacks of Washington, D.C., and the contrabands while also blocking recruitment from either population as per Stanton's desire. He refused to entertain any request pertaining to the northern freedmen, even those forwarded to his office from the president.[7] The passage of time also allowed Mitchell's differences with Usher to fester, arousing a state of near-paranoia in both men by the fall. If Usher could not convince Lincoln to shed the Emigration Office, he could exert control over its daily operations by inconveniencing its occupants. He redirected the Emigration Office's mail through the Interior Department's clerk room, where staffers logged and presumably read all incoming correspondence. Usher also instituted a policy of retaining documents deemed "official correspondence" in the Interior Department's general file, requiring Mitchell to request access to them.[8] Mitchell already viewed Usher with suspicion from his about-face to Hodge the previous spring. In his mind these actions validated doubts about Usher's commitment to seeing the British project through.

The colonization movement's history of attracting unscrupulous speculators already had both men on edge, and recent reports from Île à Vache showed the telltale signs of another swindle. This situation only caused Usher to seek greater oversight of Mitchell and Mitchell to view the secretary with greater distrust. Each blamed the other for the setbacks. Despite his own involvement in the negotiations with Kock, Usher likely came to view the scheme as an ill-conceived inheritance from his predecessor at the department. His prior reputation as a colonizationist no longer held any water, and the Emigration Office was quickly becoming more of a nuisance than a relic. Mitchell, once an enthusiastic advocate of Île à Vache, distanced himself from the faltering scheme and openly insinuated that Secretary Usher was in on the fraud.

Though general correspondence continued to be logged, Mitchell intercepted and closely guarded his exchanges with Hodge about the New River Lagoon colony. He initially displayed them to Lincoln alone and only reluctantly informed Usher of the developments on the proposed site after it stalled in early 1864. On October 21 the feud erupted with full fury. The last straw for Mitchell came when Usher's chief clerk, George C. Whiting, dispatched a subordinate to retrieve a set of colonization records from the Emigration Office. Though no means exist of independently verifying the allegation, Mitchell believed that a clerk in Usher's employ was intercepting private letters to him about the British project. He informed Whiting's assistant that his envelopes showed signs of tampering and declined to supply the requested records.[9]

Usher appears to have escalated the situation by seeking immediate access to all of Mitchell's papers. "The papers relating to colonization," he wrote, "are there by my authority and any other that may be hereafter received will take such direction as I may deem proper to give them." The interior secretary demanded copies of all future communications in writing. "You are also hereby directed to write no communications, as emanating from this department, touching any subject which you may suppose to be under your control without first obtaining the sanction and approval of the Secretary or the Assistant Secretary of the Interior."[10] Mitchell answered Usher the next day in a strongly worded enjoinder to cease his interference with the Emigration Office. "I have either the charge of the colonization work in this Department or I am independent of the Secretary of the Interior, and assigned here for office room." He stated his preference to retain an existing relationship with the Department of the Interior, as this was the original arrangement under Smith; however, should Usher continue to interfere with his office, he would not hesitate to take the case to the president.[11]

Historians should resist the temptation to treat Mitchell's warning as the bluster of an irate subordinate at his cabinet superior. His style made him a continuous annoyance in the department, but Mitchell had previously proven his political skill, and he had allies of his own. On October 28 Mitchell wrote his old friend Caleb Smith to state his grievance with Usher. Smith offered his sympathy in response and even encouraged Mitchell to seek Lincoln's help. "I am not unaware of the annoyances to which you are subjected, but am unable to see any means under my control by which I can aid in relieving you. It seems to me that your only remedy is with the president. Your appointment is direct from him, and I suppose he will not hesitate to adopt the means necessary to enable you to carry into effect the powers he has conferred upon you."[12] For the next several months Mitchell would tauntingly display this letter to Usher's clerks as they unsuccessfully pressed him to turn over documents.

The emigration commissioner also sought a legislative answer to his personal battles. In 1863 he called upon his friends within the Methodist organization to write a "joint letter" to the president supporting him "against unfriendly influences," naming Senator Pomeroy as an example.

The petition reached Bishop Matthew Simpson, an influential leader in the church and old acquaintance from Mitchell's days in the ministry. He asked the respondents to support a "recommend. to the change of the Emigration Department or Bureau" by statute, granting it budgetary independence from the Interior Department.[13]

Mitchell lined up allies in Congress who would presumably help him. "Senator Wright has nobly repayed the efforts I made in his behalf and Harland [*sic*] has stood by me." Joseph A. Wright, Democrat of Indiana and former governor of the Hoosier state, had employed Mitchell a decade earlier as his own administration's colonization agent. James Harlan, Republican of Iowa, was a devout Methodist and close friend of Bishop Simpson's. Although the desired legislation never came, Mitchell also had reason to hope at the time that his bureau would be removed from Usher's reach. Congress was considering at least one such bill at the time by Representative Godlove S. Orth of Indiana.[14] Early versions of the Freedmen's Bureau bill also toyed with the idea of transferring the Emigration Office into the War Department.

Appealing to the president also remained an option, as Smith suggested. Mitchell again proved his access to Lincoln by obtaining an audience at the White House for officers of Garnet's African Civilization Society in November 1863. The delegation's stated purpose for the meeting was only tangentially related to colonization.[15] Still, Mitchell facilitated the request and evidently considered it an important component to the eventual success of the West Indies program. Surviving records say little about Mitchell's relationship with Garnet save to arrange the presidential audience, but the society's dealings with Hodge on the New River Lagoon colony and the timing of the meeting were no coincidence. The society first approached Mitchell in September, not long after the Emigration Office announced its partnership with the British colonies in the press and only days apart from Menard's return to New York from his fact-finding mission in Belize.

As Mitchell repeatedly told Lincoln, he desired a "trustworthy body of colored men" to advise his office and lend credibility to its colonization efforts. He undoubtedly knew of Anderson's visit to Garnet's church and of Hodge's work with the society to prepare for the first wave of settlers. In his mind, a favorable conference between Lincoln and the society's delegation would shore up freedmen's support for emigration. Lack of volunteers posed a recurring problem for the administration's earlier colonization projects. Mitchell himself had great difficulty assembling a similar audience of free black leaders for Lincoln's widely reported "Address on Colonization to a Committee of Colored Men" in August 1862.[16] Garnet's organization resolved this problem and lent a strong proemigration voice from within the black community.

Ostensibly the delegation sought a meeting with Lincoln to inform him of its charitable works and present him with a request for a $5,000 "credit" from the colonization fund for projects to be administered "under the direction of colored men." Unlike the 1862 group, this delegation also came with strong attestations of support from the northern white community. They arrived with a letter signed by Henry W. Bellows, Lincoln's appointed head of the U.S. Sanitary Commission, *New York Times* editor Henry J. Raymond, railway magnate David Hoadley, and several other prominent New York citizens. The delegation left no record explicitly delineating the grant's relation to colonization, only asking that it be placed into conservatorship with the society for its general operations and educational activities. In addition to an attestation of goodwill, Mitchell likely viewed this expenditure as a seed fund to eventually stimulate the British project.[17]

Garnet remained in New York during the interview, but the delegation included George W. LeVere, his successor as the society's president, and Richard H. Cain, a Brooklyn pastor who would win election to Congress in 1872. Mitchell introduced the group at four o'clock on November 5, whereupon LeVere read a prepared statement about the organization's purpose, "the elevation of the condition of the coloured population of our own country and of other lands." Mitchell supplied Lincoln with a written copy of the address and a draft order to Usher releasing the funds to the society under the condition that they "shall lodge with [the Emigration Office] a good and sufficient bond, for the proper arrangement of those funds."[18]

Lincoln addressed the group next, though the details of his remarks do not survive. The *New York Times* reported word that he would "bestow upon their written communication due consideration." LeVere described the interview as "highly satisfactory" in a much longer speech about the meeting upon his return to New York, though it too escaped written record.[19]

Although the few public reports of this event made no explicit association between the African Civilization Society and the British projects, the meeting was clearly part of Mitchell's long-term colonization strategy. His annual report to Lincoln for 1863 identified Garnet's organization as the "proper body of discreet colored men" that had not previously "manifested itself" behind the emigration movement. This reason alone commended the group's petition, for "if emigration has to take place and money must be expended therein, equity requires that the men of color" have a directing say in its disbursement. Mitchell also deemed this expenditure more prudent than many earlier colonization efforts, which contracted the government's obligations and funds away to private bidders. Undoubtedly swayed by the recent events in Île à Vache, he stated his "reluctance to aid white men in building up private fortunes and large semi-tropical estates to be worked by colored labor at the national expense." Enlisting Garnet's help and continuing to develop the agreements with Honduras and Guiana would guard against this recurrence and provide a foundation for the future stimulation of black emigration after the war concluded.[20]

Aside from what the press reported at the time, Lincoln left little further evidence of his thoughts on the African Civilization Society's petition. Usher never released the amount on the terms requested by Mitchell, and it did not appear in the Treasury Department's final accounting of colonization expenses. Mitchell's 1864 report stated that the "aid asked could not be rendered" to the group due to "an imperfect legislation" governing the colonization fund.[21] This brief remark likely indicates that the request fell outside Usher's narrow interpretation of the enabling statutes and died from simple inattention as it, along with all colonization work, became enveloped in the emerging budgetary feud.

Mitchell's inability to secure the $5,000 grant illustrated a larger legal issue surrounding his office. He claimed that his appointment as "commissioner" included the right to administer the colonization fund in accordance with his interpretation of the president's policy, the Interior Department being obliged to affirm them. Usher in turn considered his title as only an "agent" of emigration, equivalent in rank to a department clerk and, thus, fully subordinate to the secretary's direction. The wording of Mitchell's appointment only complicated this dispute. He was already in the employ of the Interior Department as an "agent of emigration" when Congress established the colonization fund. Armed with this new resource, Lincoln gave him an amended letter of appointment and a raise in pay on August 4, 1862. The terms *commission* and *agent* both appear in the document's title. The appointment also placed his new office in "connection" with Usher's department, yet indicated that he served at the president's direction: "His office shall be in connection with the Department of the Interior, and the general duties and designs of which shall be to organize and locate colonies, superintend the immigration, settlement, or colonization of colored people of African descent under the direction of the President, who, by their own free consent may desire to migrate to countries beyond the limits of the United States, and such other general duties as may be directed by the President, on the subject of migration."[22]

Mitchell used the "agent" title prior to August 1862. After this point most government documents began referring to him as "commissioner." The latter title appears in Caleb Smith's letter to the Treasury transmitting Mitchell's pay raise and on Mitchell's own official correspondence, including the papers that Lincoln approved for Hodge and Dickson. Perhaps setting the stage for a legal case, Usher quietly reverted to using the "agent" designation sometime after his unsuccessful request to Lincoln in May 1863 seeking Mitchell's removal.

The United States Senate unwittingly reignited the feud and accompanying budget dispute on January 18, 1864, when it requested a statement of expenditures to date from the colonization fund. Usher, taking on the task as his own, asked Mitchell to prepare and "render your account to this Department for salary and other expenses incurred by you under your appointment as Agent for Colonization." The message was certainly received, and perhaps intended, as an insult. Usher exerted nearly complete control over the fund for the previous year and had receipts for all expenditures save Mitchell's salary for 1863. The interior secretary's sparing use of the fund reduced Mitchell to bearing some of his own office's clerical expenses, prompting the irascible emigration commissioner to retort: "It is unnecessary for me to state that I know little or nothing about the disbursement of the colonization fund, except what I have received as salary, as you have controlled the disbursement of that fund."[23]

Mitchell supplied an itemized budget as requested, including his salary and an additional sixty-dollar reimbursement for money given to Patrick Allen and G. W. Adrian, two Interior Department staffers he hired out of pocket to complete minor clerical and secretarial tasks. The jobs included various odds and ends over the previous year, mostly related to organizing the Emigration Office's papers and handling occasional custodial services. They represented a small fraction of the commissioner's salary, never exceeding five dollars from his monthly paycheck. Still Mitchell, already irate from the prior dispute, determined to extract every penny owed to him, while Usher met his adversary's petty accounting with a sophomoric display of his own. Mitchell's account "is approved so far as his own salary is concerned," wrote the secretary in paperwork to the Treasury. His reimbursement payments "are disallowed for the reason that those persons were in the employ of the Department, and because the payments made to them by Mr. Mitchell were not authorized by the Department and Mr. Mitchell having no authority to employ them."[24]

The Senate's review of the colonization fund hastened the need for an annual report on colonization, and both Usher and Mitchell intended to supply their own responses. As Mitchell assembled his papers he again found himself burdened by the Usher's policy of retaining documents designated "official correspondence." Since the altercation in October, Mitchell complained, "it has been your pleasure to direct [the colonization papers] away from me." This practice left Mitchell dependent upon copies of his own correspondence that were filed with Lincoln's secretaries Hay and Nicolay for the president's review.[25]

Usher intended to make a report of his own and responded in a succession of letters directing Mitchell to provide him with "all papers and correspondence in your possession having reference to the colonization of persons of African descent."[26] Mitchell took this request as yet another intrusion on his own ability to make a report and reiterated his earlier protest about access to the Interior Department files. The standoff illustrated the precarious legal circumstances of both men. Usher could control Mitchell's budget and demand his documents but could not legally force him to respond or discontinue his office without Lincoln's authorization. Cognizant of this position, the secretary could only reiterate his prior demand: "I have only to say that you will send me the papers in question without further delay, or advise me at once of your refusal to do so."[27] Mitchell relented the next day and supplied copies of his exchanges with John Hodge, the packet having been described as "private" so as to escape the secretary's "official correspondence" policy. The documents arrived with a strict enjoinder against their publication, reserved by Mitchell for use in his separate report to Congress.[28]

Usher submitted his version of the annual report to Congress on March 12.[29] The text itself consisted of a scant two pages, one of them a simple list of expenses out of the colonization fund. The document's brief narrative emphasized the Chiriquí project, abandoned over a year prior and already well known to the legislators. It contained a single short paragraph on the Île à Vache contract, glossing over the colony's problems save to note that it "proved disastrous, and it was finally determined to return the emigrants to the United States." Usher called no attention to colonization activities after an April 6, 1863, document pertaining to Île à Vache, except for itemized disbursements on the budget sheet after that date. Not one word about British Honduras, Guiana, or Lincoln's authorization to Hodge and Dickson appeared in its text.[30]

On the same day of his report Usher submitted over fifty pages of accompanying colonization records to the Senate's Committee on Territories. The bulk of this package consisted of documents from the better-known 1862 projects and letters pertaining to the rescue of the Île à Vache survivors. He only supplied two papers about the British project: his May 11 letter refusing the proposed BHC contract and revoking Hodge's privilege to visit the contrabands camp and a reiteration of Stanton's opposition from a few weeks later. In his defense, Usher had been excluded from the finer details of the West Indies negotiations through Mitchell's intransigence. He was being less than forthright to Congress though. The previous October, Usher had written the State Department to inquire about the progress that had been made on the port proclamations with Lyons. Seward's answer, which apprised him of the finalized agreement, was nowhere to be found in Usher's package.[31]

A typical member of Congress, not being privy to the State Department's negotiations or the president's personal meetings, had every reason to believe that Usher's refusal on May 1863 was the government's final word. The package contained no indication of Lincoln's countermanding order from June, nothing of the State Department's finalization of the port proclamation agreement, no word of Guiana's action on the proclamation, nothing of Menard's visit to the colony, none of Hodge's reports about the New River Lagoon site, and none of the documents Mitchell begrudgingly had supplied to Usher in February.[32] Furthermore, it appears that Mitchell's secrecy and enjoinders inadvertently created the pretext Usher needed to withhold these important papers from Congress.

Judging from its response, Congress found Usher's report unsatisfactory. On March 25 Senator Lazarus Powell of Kentucky brought a resolution to the floor requesting the president to "furnish the Senate the report of the Commissioner of Emigration for 1863." Powell apparently expected Mitchell's response from the original request, and had reason to do so. Mitchell authored annual colonization reports to Congress for the previous two years, along with several other colonization pamphlets, through the Government Printing Office. The unexpected package from the Secretary of the Interior broke with this convention. Powell's motion passed by unanimous affirmation and was transmitted to Usher the same day.[33]

Word of the failing Île à Vache colony kept Congress on edge as it awaited a response to this second request, and on May 11, Senator Morton S. Wilkinson of Minnesota offered a bill to suspend all remaining colonization funds. Describing the results of the experiment off the coast of Haiti as "most hazardous and disgraceful," he asked that "no further expenditure be made in that direction." James H. Lane of Kansas counseled his colleagues not to act in haste. The Senate asked "for a report from the commissioner of emigration of the doings under these laws . . . That report is now being made out, and I understand will be tendered to the Senate in a few days." Wilkinson announced that Mitchell's report would have little effect on his vote regardless of its contents but acceded to Lane's request and withdrew the bill.[34]

Usher was plainly miffed by the Senate's rebuff. According to Mitchell, he impeded the preparation of a separate Emigration Office report by further limiting access to relevant records. He also refused to even forward the Powell resolution to the Emigration Office, and two months passed before Mitchell received a copy. With the session winding down, an increasingly impatient Senate resubmitted its request for Mitchell's report to the Interior Department on June 22.[35]

Mitchell learned of the request independently and sent a letter to every senator save Pomeroy, informing them of his situation with Usher. "It is due to the Senate and writer to say that this resolution, although called for and the call regularly forwarded to the Department of the Interior, has never been sent to me for a report. I have such a report as my imperfect files would enable me to make, the most valuable files, such as those relating to Chiriqui and other contracts, having been withdrawn from my office. With your permission I will publish the report at the opening of the next session."[36]

After months of ignoring the resolution Usher responded with a tersely worded answer of his own on June 29. He resurrected the old dispute over Mitchell's title, "agent" or "commissioner," to justify his inaction. "I have the honor to state, that I am not aware of the existence of any such office as that of "Commissioner of Emigration", and consequently that no such official document as that alluded to by the resolution of the Senate has been or could have been made." Usher's credibility strained with each sentence. "No further agreements have since been entered into" beyond the Chiriquí and Île à Vache projects described in his March report "and no further efforts made, looking to the colonization of persons of African descent beyond the limits of the United States." The Senate, he insisted, had received all there was to know of colonization in 1863 from the documents accompanying his own March report, with neither Mitchell nor his office possessing anything further to communicate. Usher supplied the letter to Lincoln evidently intending its transmission to the Senate, but for unknown reasons the president never forwarded the document.[37]

Mitchell apparently spent the next several days hastily assembling a report of his own. He submitted a summary of his office's work to Lincoln in late June, accompanied by correspondence from Belize and a letter detailing his predicament and stating that many of his papers had been "taken herefrom, and placed by the Secty. [of the Interior] I know not where." The attachments have since separated from the cover letter, though their contents almost certainly mirror an amended report that Mitchell filed later in the year. The document typified Mitchell's style. He provided an eminently practical description of the negotiations of the British Honduras and Guiana projects, commendable to Congress as the colonies would bear the expenses of transport, then trailed off into abstract fatalistic ramblings about colonization fulfilling a supposed "destiny." Mitchell was not a man for brevity. He identified the War Department as his greatest obstacle and relayed several letters from the BHC indicating that the military routinely prevented the company's efforts to canvass the contrabands. He concluded by asking both the president and Congress to remove this impediment.[38]

Neither had the opportunity to act on Mitchell's request. Congress was in the process of rescinding Mitchell's budget, apparently at Usher's own instigation. Though long acknowledged in the colonization literature, the reasons for Congress's repeal of the colonization fund have never been fully examined. This decision is usually linked to the Île à Vache rescue, widely perceived as the final straw that proved colonization was unworkable. While the events in Haiti undoubtedly soured many legislators on colonization, its eventual demise was largely born of the budgetary fight raging around the Emigration Office.[39]

On June 25, Senator Wilkinson managed to attach a rider repealing the colonization fund to Congress's massive Sundry Civil Expenses Bill for 1865. Usher certainly welcomed the amendment as its instigator, if not an unidentified coauthor. Before offering his motion to the Senate, Wilkinson remarked in passing that he "submitted this proposition to the Secretary of the Interior" who "said it was right and ought to be passed."[40] Despite being known as a colonizationist member of the cabinet during the early part of his term, Usher was evidently willing to abandon his own stake in this policy if it rid him of Mitchell. In fact, there is very little evidence that he actively pursued colonization at all after his puzzling turnabout on Hodge's proposal in May 1863.

The Wilkinson amendment initiated a brief albeit telling debate. Senator Thomas Hendricks of Indiana sympathized with Mitchell's position and urged more time to obtain and consider his report. Henry Wilson of Massachusetts seized the opportunity to denounce the "folly" of colonization, even inserting a dig at Montgomery Blair's speeches on the subject.

James Lane of Kansas defended Mitchell's character as "unimpeachable" but favored the amendment with the view that the fund would be transferred into a newly proposed domestic colonization scheme in west Texas. Several senators concurred with Hendricks's request to eventually obtain Mitchell's report, Lane among them. In a premonition of things to come, the discussion briefly turned to whether the amendment also repealed Mitchell's salary and impeded his ability to complete the desired report. Leaving this final question open, the Senate hastily gave their assent to Wilkinson and moved on to the next amendment to the growing budget bill, an unrelated transfer of funds in the patent commissioner's account.[41]

Except for the parties involved on the Senate floor, the repeal of the colonization fund generally escaped notice. Lincoln signed the voluminous and multifaceted budget but made no public acknowledgment of its relation to the fund. His silence stands in marked contrast to longstanding interpretations of the budget bill and its assumed connection to the Île à Vache rescue mission. In private, Congress's action likely precipitated John Hay's famous diary passage on July 1, 1864, noting that Lincoln had "sloughed off that idea of colonization." Whether Hay reached this conclusion from a conversation with the president or by simple inference from the bill, his timing suggests that the White House was made cognizant of Wilkinson's clause, buried deep within the bill, when Lincoln affixed his signature. Still, Lincoln's approval of a massive budget containing a hastily inserted anticolonization amendment does not carry the interpretive weight that it would from a stand-alone proposition. Did Lincoln personally concur with rescinding the fund by mid 1864? Or did he deem it a temporary concession, knowing that the colonization policy was stalled at the time and likely would be until the war's end? He left little indication either way.

The meaning of Hay's peculiar terminology has similarly been a source of speculation for decades, its occasion often being used to signify Lincoln's evolving racial beliefs and abandonment of colonization once and for all.[42] The British projects of the previous year temper this conclusion insofar as Hay had no direct involvement in the BHC negotiations, despite his closeness to the president. His later historical writings with Nicolay illustrate this through their unfortunate effect of pigeonholing a century of subsequent scholarship to Chiriquí and Île à Vache, not because these were the only ventures Lincoln pursued but because the presidential secretaries seem to have known of little else beyond them.[43]

If any meaning is to be read into Lincoln's signature on the Sundry Civil Expenses Bill, the context of the Usher-Mitchell feud suggests a simpler explanation. Lincoln succumbed to frustration with his subordinates and the corruption that colonization seemed to attract. Hay implies as much, noting that "I have always thought [colonization] a hideous & barbarous humbug & thievery of Pomeroy and Kock," recipient of the Île à Vache contract, "have about converted him to the same belief." Hay made this entry following a conversation with Mitchell, who claimed that Usher had confiscated the Emigration Office's records to allow Pomeroy to "cook up his fraudulent accounts by."[44] And as Mitchell was quick to argue to any who would listen, the failures on Usher's watch provided all the more reason to extend greater autonomy to the Emigration Office.

While its signals on the future of colonization under Lincoln may be less clear than originally thought, the Wilkinson amendment did produce one immediate and tangible effect. Usher used it as a pretext to retroactively rescind Mitchell's salary, halting payments as of January 1, 1864, the last date acknowledged in his March report. Unbeknownst to him at the time, Usher would have to endure another year of this burdensome subordinate. Though operating without a paycheck, Mitchell retained his title and appointment and had every intention of claiming the monies due to him. Wilkinson, too, may have botched the language of his amendment. As Mitchell readily pointed out, an earlier law still remained on the books and dedicated a fixed portion of tax revenues from seized lands in insurrectionary states "to aid in the colonization or emigration from said State of any free person of African descent who may desire to remove therefrom to Hayti, Liberia, or any other tropical state or colony."[45] If not from the colonization fund, he would seek his funding from this source and do so free of Usher's control.

In practical terms though, the Wilkinson amendment effectively concluded American participation in the British emigration projects. Mitchell still pressed for their revival, and other colonization schemes emerged from time to time, including Lane's proposal for west Texas. Still, the United States government's last realistic attempt at colonization was all but a dead letter. More significant, it was not finished off as part of a preconceived strategy, meticulously executed to palliate a reluctant public. Nor did it outwardly signify a dramatic "change of heart" in Lincoln's colonization philosophy, bound by unwavering consistency and driven by sweeping ethical goals; only his reaction to an ongoing political nuisance. The impetus behind the British Honduras and Guiana projects succumbed to a simple yet pronounced breakdown in bureaucratic government as the conflicting interests, agendas, and personalities of the agents involved overtook the policies they were assigned to administer.

Chapter 9

The Indefatigable James Mitchell

Despite his budgetary setbacks James Mitchell continued to press for the British emigration scheme's revival in the United States. On November 24, 1864, he submitted his promised supplement to the report sought by the Senate in June, hoping that Congress would act to restore his funding in the approaching winter session. He asked Congress to directly appropriate the $5,000 "credit" requested by the African Civilization Society and expressed hope of resuming work on the British Honduras and Guiana projects, noting both colonies still desired labor.[1]

Mitchell enclosed a supplement, wherein he lashed out at the Chiriquí and Île à Vache contracts. These ventures ignored "the true interests of the emigrant" in pursuit of the "personal emolument of the parties" involved. Though he avoided naming Usher directly, he attributed the failure of both schemes to the actions of "sundry parties not responsible" for the Emigration Office's work and beyond its jurisdiction. Should Congress resume colonization, he urged that it be placed in the hands of "reliable agencies" such as the British colonies or handled through direct dealings with the governments of Haiti and Liberia.[2]

The intervening months since Congress had repealed the colonization fund had done little to alleviate the raging animosity between Mitchell and Usher. On the contrary, Congress's action had introduced new legal ambiguities. Mitchell asserted on a reasonably strong legal basis that even though his budget was repealed, he retained a commission to his office from Lincoln. This authorized him to make the supplemental report, which several senators had expected the previous June even as they voted to abolish the colonization fund.[3] Usher's retroactive suspension of Mitchell's salary to January 1864 only further complicated the issue by tapping into an authorized portion of the fund, and it set the stage for a protracted legal battle.

Mitchell traveled west to visit his family during the summer's congressional recess, briefly pausing to write Lincoln about his political troubles.

The journey likely reignited his flair for Hoosier politics, which may have also been the original source of his bitterness with Usher. Both men were veterans of a tumultuous political battle in the 1850s over the future of free blacks in Indiana, one of the most "negrophobic" northern states, and may have crossed paths as part of rival Republican and Democratic factions.[4] The emigration commissioner attributed Usher's "foolish war on me" to "the instigation of the Arch-traytor [*sic*] Elwood Fisher years ago, and continued by the direction of an equally pure cliant [*sic*] A. W. Thompson," the recipient of the original Chiriquí contract. Wrote Mitchell, "I respectfully and earnestly urge a change in the Department of the Interior" after the fall election, and he suggested that his own replacement come from the Midwest.[5]

Unbeknownst to the president, Mitchell was simultaneously plotting to oust Usher through the influence of his old friend Bishop Matthew Simpson. Even without Mitchell's schemes, Usher's job was imperiled by the arrival of Hugh McCulloch as the new treasury secretary at the outset of Lincoln's second term. This appointment left Indiana overrepresented on the cabinet, and Simpson sensed a chance to push for a Methodist nominee. A few days before the November election Mitchell wrote Simpson about their strategy to replace Usher. He advised the bishop to avoid pressing Lincoln on any other political appointments. "It will take all the power we can muster to force our member of Cabinet on the Govt. and if you and others reserve their strength we will likely succeed."[6]

Simpson, Mitchell, and Lincoln each had multiple reasons to favor the intended replacement, Iowa Senator James Harlan. He was a personal friend of Lincoln's (his daughter would later marry the president's son Robert). Simpson had also known the Harlan family for years through their membership in his church, and the Methodist connection similarly appealed to Mitchell. More important, Harlan was sympathetic to Mitchell's recent difficulties in the Interior Department.

By November 1864 Usher's replacement was a forgone conclusion due to the elevation of McCulloch in Treasury. Lincoln named Harlan to the Interior post, owing in part to Simpson's lobbying.[7] The changeover would prove a slow and painful one, illustrating Usher's coldness toward his successor. Though Lincoln secured Usher's resignation almost immediately after the November election, the new appointment would not take effect until after Inauguration Day the next spring. According to Harlan's principal biographer, Usher used this period to stack the department payroll with "the names of many newspaper correspondents and protégés of

Congressmen. The service of these men were more or less perfunctory, or at most, fell far short of the expectations and demands of the department's new head."[8]

Harlan's friendship with Mitchell likely did little to help the transition, and Usher appears to have placed the blame for his termination on the Methodist organization. Some months into his tenure the new interior secretary complained in a letter about his predecessor "making a personal and malignant war on me." He also wrote Bishop Simpson about the problems he inherited at the department: "[I]t is exceedingly difficult to change the organs of a vast business in a day. I have changed the worst ones."[9]

The matter of Mitchell's garnished wages and future job security played a central role in the transition. Mitchell first approached Lincoln for help in recovering his earnings shortly after returning from Indiana in September 1864. He presented the president with a copy of Smith's letter from the previous December and accompanying documents pertaining to his accounts, which Usher had completely frozen.[10]

It is difficult to know Lincoln's personal position, but he certainly was aware of the feud and appears to have been sympathetic to Mitchell's case. He acted on Mitchell's request almost immediately upon its receipt, promptly asking for an opinion from Attorney General Bates on September 9. The accompanying note likely contained the president's last written word on the subject of colonization, but it is inaccessible, likely one of the valuable documents lost in a fire that ravaged Bates's personal papers some years later. The only surviving record of its contents is a brief clerk's note from the attorney general's log book:

> Sept. 9th The Presd.
> Requesting opin as to whether provsn's of Cong. for colonization of colored persons have ceased & whether office of Comm. of Emigration continues.

The request also contained a copy of Mitchell's petition, personally "endorsed" by Lincoln and "requesting opinion of the Atty. Genl. on points above mentioned to be ordered by Presd."[11]

The attorney general's answer came slowly, presumably owing to Bates's own impending retirement. Mitchell inquired again about the fate of his office on October 20, asking "[i]f the Attorney General rules that my present position is not tenable, be so kind as to grant me one more . . . [m]y means being slender." He enclosed a "paper some friends tendered on learning whilst at home that the appropriation for my office had been repealed," now lost, and expressed his thanks to Lincoln "for what you have done."[12]

Bates's reply finally arrived on November 30, though time did not permit him to answer every legal question surrounding Mitchell's status. The attorney general tendered his own resignation the same day, making the opinion on the Emigration Office one of his last official acts. The letter is styled as a response to "your question concerning your power still to retain the Revd Mr Mitchell as your assistant or aid in the matter of executing the several acts of Congress relating to the emigration or Colonizing of the freed blacks." Bates answered, "I can only say that, having examined all the acts referred to, I am satisfied that, notwithstanding the act which repeals the appropriation contingently, you still have *something* to do, under those acts; and therefore, that you have the same right to continue Mr Mitchell that you had to appoint him originally. And I hope it will be done, for he seems to be a good man, of zeal & capacity."[13]

Armed with this paper and a recommendation from Harlan, Mitchell presented his claim to the Treasury Department and received his back pay through the previous June.[14] The remainder of Mitchell's request, including his salary after July 2, 1864, and the future status of his office, persisted without resolution until after Lincoln's assassination.

Mitchell's case for resuming his position rested heavily on the support of incoming Interior Secretary James Harlan. He wrote Simpson in March to "rejoice that the effort to place Senator Harlan in the Cabinet has been a success." Regrettably though, the new secretary's "commission does not begin to him before the 15th of May." In the same letter he lamented to the bishop about his own future. "I presume I will be obliged to abandon the field for the present," citing "broken pledges, broken laws, broken truth and expectations."[15]

Harlan made the Emigration Office one of his first priorities after his appointment took effect and began seeking a legal avenue to reinstate Mitchell. As he noted to James Speed, the new attorney general, "[i]t does not appear from the records of this department that the President's letter of appointment has ever been revoked." Speed reviewed the case and advised Harlan that he could not legally pay Mitchell for any work done after the colonization fund's repeal. The appointment notwithstanding, the new attorney general opined that Mitchell's salary was tied by law to the revoked colonization account and had therefore ceased on June 30, 1864, the last day covered by the Bates opinion. The Emigration Office was effectively no more.[16]

Mitchell continued his tireless pursuit of the British Honduras project through the fall of 1865, seeking to revive it by public campaign. He wrote Seward in September to "respectfully suggest that the completion of the combination once proposed with England may now be effected to a great extent."[17] The same month, in an interview with a reporter from the *New York Times,* he urged Congress to resume the British projects. He also published a pamphlet promoting his work and claiming that colonial authorities were to "this day asking me to fulfill their engagement." Honduras and Guiana no longer awaited American freedmen as their only source of labor, as, by this time, the project had little realistic chance for revival in the United States, but Mitchell's statement probably contained a grain of truth nonetheless. Even at this late date both colonies would no doubt accept workers should they become available in the future or so they had informed the British Legation in Washington. As late as October 1865, the BHC even notified its shareholders that "skilled and free negro labourers are looked for from the United States."[18]

Mitchell displayed an almost incorrigible trait for testing the waters for colonization at opportune points, appealing to President Johnson in 1865 for the creation of a new colonization office to outlast the Freedmen's Bureau.[19] He similarly called upon the State Department and Congress alike to "fulfill" Abraham Lincoln's policy. Lincoln was a convenient, if not valuable, ally to enlist to the colonization cause, and Mitchell made liberal use of his former employer's name, but not even a martyred president's memory could revivify the scheme. The Republican Party in Congress had moved beyond its Whiggish origins, its membership now augmented by an emboldened group of Radicals. Legislators who once entertained colonization as a way to keep the slave population from moving north after emancipation suddenly found partisan uses for maintaining a southern voting bloc in the free black community.[20] Even though Lincoln had come out of the older Henry Clay Whig tradition, the Radicals laid their own claim to his legacy, and Mitchell's pleas to Congress were ignored. The former emigration commissioner eventually resigned himself to the inevitable. He held out until 1866, occasionally asking Harlan if the Interior Department would hire him to revive its colonization work. His monies exhausted and requests declined, Mitchell returned to the Methodist ministry.[21]

In an interesting parallel, Mitchell's former clerk J. Willis Menard initially displayed a similar reluctance to abandon his interest in emigration. Perhaps encouraged by his experience in British Honduras, Menard—together with his Jamaican-born wife, Elizabeth—briefly relocated to Jamaica in 1865.

But his hopes of finding a new home in the West Indies were replaced by frustration as he observed the impoverished conditions of Jamaica's "free-labor" plantation system firsthand. "The prosperity and happiness of our race and their posterity lay in a separation from the white race" thundered a pamphlet that he distributed to black laborers. British colonial authorities were none too pleased by this foreign agitator from the United States. October 1865 saw the brutal suppression of the Morant Bay rebellion by Governor Eyre after black laborers rose up in protest against poor economic conditions and discriminatory suffrage laws. Believing him connected to the uprising, Eyre had Menard escorted under armed guard to the U.S. Consulate at Kingston and ordered him deported. Menard's American citizenship likely saved him from the firing squad that claimed Paul Bogle and George William Gordon.[22]

The experience clearly had a disillusioning effect on Menard's support for immigration to the British empire. He returned to New Orleans and quickly refocused his energies on bettering the condition of blacks within the U.S. political system. In 1868, J. Willis Menard became the first African American to win election to the United States Congress. His victory at the polls generated much fanfare in the press, and in early 1869 he addressed the House of Representatives, but the body refused to seat him when a white opponent challenged the election results. According to reports at the time, future president James A. Garfield deemed it too early to admit an African American to Congress, even if he won a majority at the ballot box. Menard persisted in politics though, eventually winning a seat in the Florida legislature and becoming a prominent Republican organizer in that state.[23] He never fully relinquished his colonizationist views. As late as 1878, he still held out hope for an emigration movement to Haiti or Liberia. "Let them venture everywhere, as the whites do," he urged an audience of black citizens in Washington. The violence and politics of Reconstruction had taken their toll.[24]

James Mitchell's later life is noteworthy as well, not only for his career, but for its significance to the Emigration Office's sporadic paper trail. With Congress's interest in colonization exhausted, the displaced Emigration Commissioner refocused his energies on the Methodist church. Mitchell made note of this new direction in a diary entry: "My work in Washington being brought to an untimely close by the tragic events surrounding the death of President Lincoln, I wished to return to the ministry and decided to volunteer for ministerial work in the South."[25]

In 1866 Mitchell reentered the clergy under the guidance of his father-in-law, Levi Scott, a senior bishop in the United States Methodist organization. His assignment to a church in Leesburg, Virginia, a town on the banks of the Potomac just north of Washington, D.C., kept him moving in or near the same political circles he had traveled as Lincoln's colonization officer. The evidence is strong that many of Mitchell's old political friends still held him in high regard, despite the feud with Usher and his sometimes overbearing personality traits. In late 1865, during a trip west to St. Louis, he called upon Edward Bates, the former attorney general, and the two talked politics for several hours.[26] His diary also referenced frequent encounters with old friends from Washington during his clergy assignments after the war.

Mitchell could not let go of the belief that he had been cheated out of some of his salary by Usher's machinations. Writing to President Grant in 1871 in another attempt to claim a final year's worth of pay, he left behind some intriguing details of the last days of his office. True to form he alluded all too scantily to events which might well have occurred but for which there can be little independent verification. Mitchell reported that around the time the Freedmen's Bureau was being organized in 1865, he had been "thought to expect its control on sundry grounds" and had maintained his own office from summer 1864 for roughly a year, largely due to the assurance of something better to come.

But the "inequitable and unreasonable" New England faction demanded "entire control of the Negro Question." Chancing upon bureau director Oliver O. Howard when collecting some of his papers, Mitchell learned the political situation and received an offer of a "subordinate place," though only if he provided his own desks and clerks. Mitchell considered this the last straw in "a series of proscriptive measures, that left me with no alternative but to quietly and loyally step aside and let others direct the matter." Considering this the effective end of his work for the government, he demanded his wages from July 1, 1864, when they had ceased to be paid under the terms restored by Bates's opinion, to June 1, 1865, about the time of Howard's appointment. Reducing $1,800 per annum to $1,650 in pro-rata terms, since this period had not quite been a year, he then suggested remuneration with interest at 6 percent annually to produce a demand of $2,226.75.[27]

Undoubtedly aware that the Treasury Department was still attempting to finalize the colonization fund accounts some five years later amidst rumors of its misuse, Mitchell took another passing swipe at Pomeroy and Usher. What justice could there be in a system that allowed "a Senator and his friends to hold and use Twenty-five Thousand Dollars . . . of the

Colonization funds, without accomplishing any thing to justify such a draft on the Treasury" while denying the government's principal colonization administrator simple compensation for his salaried work? Perhaps he hoped to convince Grant that colonization faltered through the scheming of others should it ever be entertained again as policy. Tantalizingly, Mitchell also informed Grant that he held in his personal possession more official government papers than he could find time to copy, which had been boxed up with his own when he had expected to move from the Interior Department to the War Department.[28]

Senator Charles Sumner also wrote Mitchell at his church in Leesburg from time to time. One exchange from 1871 returned to the subject of colonization under Lincoln. The Massachusetts legislator was researching the history of U.S. land policies in the Caribbean while mounting his opposition to an attempt by President Grant to annex Santo Domingo, intended in part to serve as a home for ex-slaves. Sumner asked for Mitchell's knowledge of "any opinions expressed by President Lincoln on colonization or empire in the West Indies." Specifically, "did he think those islands the proper home of the colored race, rather than the white race?" "And did he think annexation desirable?" The former orchestrator of the British Honduras scheme described Lincoln's position and, purportedly, the late president's intention for a second term. "He did not covet them as part of our dominion, quite otherwise, but desired that England should unite with us in creating an independent colored commonwealth in the American tropics for the benefit of the colored race and the relief of the south."[29] It is unclear if Sumner made use of this information, and any response, if tendered, likely disappeared with Mitchell's personal papers, but the Santo Domingo treaty faltered amidst Senate opposition.

These privately offered remarks, solicited by Sumner, likely marked the end of the former emigration commissioner's involvement in colonization politics. Mitchell's career in the ministry eventually landed him in rural Georgia where he took a leadership post in the church hierarchy. He established a chain of religious schools under the Methodist conference's instructions to provide educational opportunities for the impoverished "white youths of this section" and oversaw efforts to forge ties with the religious schools of the separate African Methodist Episcopal Church.[30] Perhaps he saw schooling as a practical necessity in his adopted state and recognized its tangible benefits to both races. Even at the peak of his colonization career Mitchell had never shied away from the black community where their goals aligned. Now that goal was education.

James Mitchell nonetheless maintained until the end of his life that Lincoln intended to carry the British projects through in his second term. An engraving of Francis Carpenter's "The First Reading of the Emancipation Proclamation" hung on his office wall at the Mt. Zion Seminary, the school he founded and administered in Carroll County, Georgia. He greeted the occasional visitor, often one seeking Lincoln anecdotes, by pointing to the engraving and stating "that is strictly a colonization document." Many valuable papers from his work as emigration commissioner, including now-lost exchanges with Hodge and letters in Lincoln's own hand, sat a few feet away from his desk, the relocated relics of his confrontation with Usher some three decades prior. At least Mitchell's will indicated as much. He specifically asked that his "African and Colonization books and State Papers" be set aside from his library, "undivided" in the hope that they would be used for a suitable history of "the troubles of the past, when the negro question dominated all others."[31]

The collection was reportedly large, filling the many boxes of official and private correspondence that Mitchell had described to Grant several decades prior. It undoubtedly contained the primary American records from the British Honduras project, including those withheld from Usher as the two men dueled for control of the colonization fund. Mitchell also likely retained one of two recorded originals from the 1863 port proclamation order signed by Lincoln, to say nothing of other lost correspondence with senators, cabinet members, and, conceivably, the president himself. Excepting a short biography authored by his great-niece and printed as a pamphlet by the school, no project materialized from the colonization papers, and these valuable documents passed into history with Mitchell's death in 1903.[32]

Chapter 10

Colonization Repudiated, Colonization Revived?

Abraham Lincoln left little direct indication of his final disposition on the emigration projects in British Honduras or any other Caribbean locale. The president indisputably sustained the schemes throughout 1863, including against the internal resistance of his cabinet. He pitched the West Indies scheme to Lyons at its outset in January, revived it in June when Usher and Stanton declined Hodge's offer, and prodded a reluctant State Department to finalize the agreement with the British Legation in August. Mitchell claimed Lincoln's support for the project in his private letters and public newspaper articles alike throughout the fall of 1863 and probably with credence. Lincoln still valued Mitchell's counsel as shown by the African Civilization Society meeting in November. By June 1864 though, Mitchell was pleading for Lincoln's response to unanswered letters from Hodge.[1] Had political wrangling finally exhausted Lincoln's patience for colonization? Or was he simply occupied with other, more pressing matters of the raging war?

If Lincoln moved away from colonization in the summer of 1864, he did so by simple inattention as the Mitchell-Usher feud overshadowed and consumed any meaningful work on the Caribbean projects. Lincoln intervened to assist Mitchell with his salary but left little indication that he intended to rescue the scheme from his subordinates' mishandling yet again. But neither did Lincoln ever conclusively distance himself from colonization—a point that was not lost upon his adversaries in Congress.

Lincoln had many opportunities to publicly reject his prior colonizationist position; indeed, by 1864 it might have been politically advantageous to do so. Montgomery Blair continued to espouse colonization on the president's behalf, as did his brother, a congressman from Missouri. In early 1864, echoing the postmaster general a few months prior, Representative Frank Blair publicly identified colonization, carried out in conjunction with emancipation, as the administration's official policy.[2]

Historians have generally downplayed the Blairs' influence at this point in Lincoln's presidency, their remarks amounting to little more than bluster from the cabinet's conservative faction.[3] Montgomery left his post in September 1864 as part of a compromise to stave off a challenge to Lincoln's reelection from the Radical Republican wing of his own party. His resignation was voluntarily offered and apparently accepted with reluctance by Lincoln, who had repeatedly rebuffed the Radicals' prior calls to sack the postmaster general.[4]

Equally significant, Lincoln had endured over a year of vocal hostility against the Blair family from the Radicals, much of it tied directly to colonization. Radical agitation boiled over in October 1863 when Montgomery Blair delivered another bombastic assault on the "abolition" wing of the Republican Party in Rockville, Maryland. The speech avoided explicitly enlisting colonization but echoed his critiques of Stanton from the early summer in which colonization had been a recurring theme.[5] The British Honduras project he had helped to craft in June was probably on his mind at the time, as the War Department remained an impediment to the recruitment of the contrabands. By winter it was Frank's turn to retort the Radicals on their reconstruction agenda, and he made colonization a centerpiece of his counterattack in Congress.

Though the colonization program retained its appeal to many moderate Republicans, it had fallen from favor among most Radicals by 1864. They had come to despise the Blair family's influence with the president and with it their pet project of colonization. Others simply recognized its inconsistency with an emerging strain of egalitarianism in the Republican Party. Senator Henry Wilson complained to Lincoln of the postmaster general's speeches, which were being circulated in the name of the administration yet were "universally denounced in New England." The Rockville speech in particular drew the ire of such men as Representative Thaddeus Stevens and Senator Charles Sumner, and prompted a Republican newspaperman to demand Blair's resignation in Lincoln's presence.[6]

Undeterred, the Blairs met their critics in force and openly claimed to speak on behalf of the president himself. On February 5, 1864, Frank Blair delivered a tirade against Stevens and accused the ill-tempered Pennsylvanian of intentionally subverting the administration with radical reconstruction and racial policies. The president, he insisted, wished for emancipation to be carried out with "compensation for slaves in the loyal Border states, and colonization of the freedmen in some suitable locality."[7] As with previous Blair speeches, the Radicals were incensed and none more so than Representative

Henry Winter Davis of Maryland, who considered Frank to be little more than the president's appointed surrogate in Congress. This characterization overstated Lincoln's direct involvement, although he was undoubtedly aware of Frank's speech. Montgomery personally supplied him with a copy at the cabinet meeting a few days later.[8]

Davis had a long-boiling personal distaste for both the Blairs and Lincoln, perhaps inspired in part by the belief that he had been snubbed for a cabinet position in Montgomery's favor. Convinced that Lincoln was "thoroughly Blairized," the irascible congressman rose on the House floor on February 25, 1864, to answer Frank with colonization serving as his intended stratagem for dividing the president from the cabinet's conservatives.[9] In no uncertain terms Davis demanded that Lincoln repudiate the Blairs and abandon colonization once and for all. Frank Blair intended his remarks as a broadside against the radicals, Davis contended, but their "substance is a vindication of the colonization policy." Blair's position, he continued, could only be interpreted as the president's own. "Those comments have never been disavowed. They are entitled to our grave and respectful consideration, both from the high position and character of the gentleman from whom they emanate, and his peculiar relations to the President, and the concurrence of view between him and the President asserted and not disavowed."[10]

The Republican press took notice of the speech and circulated it in pamphlet form. Davis privately bragged of his intent to Rear Admiral Samuel F. Du Pont, a friend and confidant who had also recently soured on the administration. "I hung around his neck his colonization folly weighted with Blair's worse comments; if he can swim with that he is very light."[11]

Davis was a loose cannon even among the Radicals but a source of political irritation nonetheless, and his speech presented a public opportunity for Lincoln to dissociate himself from colonization. His challenge made a stir in Congress and almost certainly reached the president's desk. Lincoln gave no answer.

Frank Blair did, though, by seizing on the earliest chance to respond from the House floor. In ever-bolder language, the Missouri congressman identified colonization as "Mr. Lincoln's humane, wise, and benevolent policy." "Is it not better," he queried, "for the negroes to have provided a country for them in which they can govern themselves by their own laws, in which they will have no superiors" though they would enjoy the protection of the United States government?[12] Blair's remarks targeted the radicals, or "Jacobins" as he called them, over more than colonization. He dissected their proposed reconstruction policies, reiterated his call for compensated emancipation in the border states, and accused the Republican leadership in Congress of betraying the policies of the president.

Furious, the Radicals reacted swiftly. They challenged the validity of Blair's most recent reelection to Congress and initiated an investigation to hear a challenge from his opponent. One observer even wrote Lincoln from the House gallery before the speech was over, asking him to renounce Blair, who surely "missrepresents you."[13] Shortly after the speech Blair quietly returned to a military command in the Union army with the president's assent. As to the matter of colonization, Lincoln still gave no answer.

Lincoln weathered the Blairs' storm without as much as a single word for his critics. He answered neither the specific challenge of Davis on colonization nor the general complaints from the Radicals. Beyond the claims of their speeches and the knowledge that Lincoln was aware of them, it is difficult to ascertain the degree to which the Blairs still represented the administration in 1864. But it is equally certain that Lincoln chose to forgo a public opportunity to repudiate them on colonization or any other issue despite intense pressure to do so. Congress did not hesitate to read an endorsement into this silence. As Representative James A. Garfield quipped in reference to Frank, "Lincoln's creature was sent here for a special purpose, which, when accomplished, he put him back in his place, thus ratifying all he said and did when here."[14]

The only recorded instance where Lincoln may have expressed his doubts on colonization occurred in private several months later—the famous Hay diary passage. Notably, the presidential secretary attributed the July 1864 "slough[ing] off" to Lincoln's frustration with the failure of his colonization attempts and the corruption they seemed to attract rather than a philosophical reckoning. His observation is consistent with Congress's decision to repeal the funds a few days prior. Colonization ceased not at Lincoln's instigation, but by an act of Congress born of their frustrations with the Mitchell-Usher feud and fed by Usher's apparent willingness to cede the colonization budget as a means of removing Mitchell.

Although Hay attributed some finality to Lincoln's move away from the policy, several of Lincoln's associates apparently believed that he would revive colonization after the war when he could give it greater attention. Gideon Welles later described Lincoln as "disappointed" by the failure of his administration's colonization experiments. Yet he "by no means abandoned his policy of deportation and emancipation, for the two were in his mind indispensably and indissolubly connected. Colonization in fact had precedence with him."[15] Henry Clay Whitney, an old Illinois acquaintance of the president's, made a similar observation. "Lincoln was a colonizationist, as Jefferson, Madison and Henry Clay were; and he attempted in several ways, as I show, to engraft that policy on his administration as a practical measure, and would have made still more heroic efforts, looking to that end, had he completed his second term."[16]

Others still speculated about the oft-stated relationship between colonization and the Emancipation Proclamation. Welles "doubted whether he would not have hesitated longer in issuing the decree of emancipation had he been aware that colonization would not be accepted as an accompaniment." Congressman George Julian openly wondered "that if the President had foreseen" the failure of colonization "his preliminary notice to the rebels would have been given."[17] Samuel Pomeroy gave a comparable assessment in an 1889 speech on the anniversary of Lincoln's death. "The only outlet for the African race, in Lincoln's opinion, was to free them and colonize them in the tropics. Lincoln had no idea that the negroes were to live among us as freedmen with equal rights."[18]

The most famous and contentious suggestion that Lincoln intended to revive colonization appears in the autobiographical reminiscences of Benjamin F. Butler, a Union army "political general" out of Massachusetts who had a habit of finding himself in the middle of controversy. Late in his life, General Butler related an anecdote about a "colonization interview" he allegedly held with Lincoln a few days before the president's assassination. According to Butler, a "very much disturbed" Lincoln approached him on an April morning in 1865 and asked "what shall we do with the negroes after they are free?" Anticipating that the freed slaves would "be but little better off with their masters than they were before," he settled upon the resumption of colonization. "I can hardly believe that the South and North can live in peace, unless we can get rid of the negroes . . . I believe that it would be better to export them all to some fertile country with a good climate, which they could have to themselves."[19]

The two men discussed the logistics of this scheme, eventually settling on a plan to colonize the Isthmus of Darien and employ the freedmen in the construction of a ship canal. During the war Butler oversaw the digging of the Dutch Gap canal on the James River, an ultimately unsuccessful effort to bypass Confederate defensive positions guarding Richmond. He suggested utilizing his own experience from this project and deploying the enlisted men of the United States Colored Troops to Panama to dig an interoceanic waterway. Their wives and children would follow with Congress's assistance, inducing a free migration of blacks seeking work and an escape from the discriminatory postwar South. Lincoln concluded, "[T]here is meat in that, General Butler, there is meat in that."[20] The two men then parted ways with Butler intending to follow through until John Wilkes Booth's infamous bullet struck Lincoln dead before any action could be taken.

Assuming for the moment that it is accurate, one takes Butler's anecdote to indicate that Lincoln never truly abandoned colonization. Lincoln may have "sloughed off" colonization due to the war and a contentious situation within the administrative bureaucracy, but perhaps he intended to revive it in his second term, much as Mitchell, Welles, and Whitney suggested. Butler's tale directly supports this conclusion, but is it credible?

Several newspapers found the anecdote noteworthy when Butler's story appeared in print, first in 1886 and again in 1892. One periodical categorized it among "the most interesting in the book," and another simply restated the anecdote as if it were a matter of fact.[21] These early reviews, published in Butler's own lifetime, accepted the account without reservation and addressed it only as an interesting additional detail in the life of Lincoln. Indeed, for its first few decades in print Butler's "colonization interview" became a familiar piece of Lincoln lore.[22]

Most early Lincoln scholars also accepted Butler's story with little question, but doubt began to surface as colonization became a specialized topic of inquiry in the 1950s.[23] More recent historians have deferred to the detective work of Mark E. Neely, who conducted a detailed textual scrutiny of the anecdote in 1979. Using the narrative from the 1892 autobiography and comparing it to other known historical records, Neely discovered several inconsistencies in the anecdote's timeline. In the best-known version, Butler purported to have sat for the interview at a time when he was not even in Washington, having only visited the city several days later after Lincoln departed for Virginia in late March to meet with General Ulysses S. Grant.[24] Neely also identified multiple exaggerated characteristics in the statements Butler attributed to Lincoln. Taken cumulatively, the faults in the autobiography cast doubt upon the authenticity of Butler's claims and led most historians to discount his veracity.

A recent examination of the Butler anecdote by one of the authors of the present work found that the timeline inconsistencies are likely the product of the general's faulty memory rather than willful deception. The meeting itself indisputably happened, although Butler mistook his dates by about two weeks in the 1892 autobiography. Independent corroborating documents reveal that Butler arrived at the White House on April 11, 1865, instead of March as he suggested.[25] He met with Lincoln in private, the subject of their discussion known only to its two participants. Lincoln's account, if indeed he ever told another of the interview, died with him only four days later.

Butler personally wrote a narrative of the interview for two separate publications, first a lesser-known essay for Allen Thorndike Rice's collection of Lincoln reminiscences in 1886 followed by his better-known 1892 autobiography.[26] Save for the author's own analysis, historians have focused almost exclusively on the 1892 autobiography. The story actually predates both written accounts though. In 1884 an unnamed correspondent to the *New York Times* recounted the anecdote as biographical matter in an article about the general:

> At the close of the civil war [Butler] seriously proposed to Lincoln that the United States should immediately begin the construction of an interoceanic canal across the Isthmus. He submitted his scheme to Mr. Lincoln a few days before Booth's bullet did its fatal work. In brief, it was to transport to Central America 50,000 freedmen and begin the work. . . . He saw in his mind's eye the solution of a vexatious political and social problem at home, the construction of a vast undertaking which would revolutionize the commerce of the world, and the colonization of surplus blacks in a region where they could, under competent direction, do the most for themselves and for humanity. The Government had the transports, the commissary stores, the material of war, which upon the disbandment of its great armies must be sacrificed.[27]

Butler had apparently spoken of this "colonization interview" many times before he committed it to print on his own, one example of which remarkably survived, albeit unnoticed.

Barring any new discoveries, the credibility of Butler's testimony is an open matter for interpretation and conjecture.[28] Both of Butler's versions of the anecdote display his well-known propensity for exaggeration, but also carry a hint of truth. The *New York Times* version also mirrors both later accounts, though its details are comparatively sparse. There are several reasons to doubt portions of each. Notably, the general supplied unlikely words of praise for his military ability during the James River campaign of 1864 and conveniently named himself as the visionary behind Lincoln's plan. Yet the two accounts also reflect Lincoln's contemplative approach to slavery and his well-documented fear of racial violence after the war.[29] Perhaps most telling is that Butler relayed the story multiple times, many years apart. The biggest textual discrepancies of each are in the admittedly faulty timeline. The other details exhibit a remarkable level of consistency though.

Table I: Butler's Colonization Interview – A Textual Comparison of Sources

NEW YORK TIMES (1884)	RICE, ED., REMINISCENCES (1886)
Date: Before April 14, 1865: "[Butler] submitted his scheme to Mr. Lincoln a few days before Booth's bullet did its fatal work."	**Date:** After April 9, 1865: "Lincoln was very much disturbed after the surrender of Lee and he had been to Richmond."
	Lincoln's introduction: "General Butler, I am troubled about the negroes."
Lincoln's concern: "[Butler] saw in his mind's eye the solution of a vexatious political and social problem at home."	**Lincoln's concern:** "We got some one hundred and odd thousand who have been trained to arms." "I fear lest these colored men shall organize themselves in the South, especially in the States where the negroes are in preponderance in numbers, into guerrilla parties and we shall have down there a warfare between the whites and the negroes."
Colonization: "[Butler] saw...the colonization of surplus blacks in a region where they could, under competent direction, do the most for themselves and for humanity."	**Colonization:** (Lincoln speaking) "Would it not be possible to export them to some place say Liberia or South America and organize them into communities to support themselves?"
	Interlude: "After some few days of examination with aid of statistics and calculations of this topic I went to the President's office in the morning."
	Logistics: "[N]egro children will be born faster than your whole naval and merchant vessels if substantially all of them were devoted to that use can carry them from the country."
Butler's solution: "At the close of the civil war [Butler] seriously proposed to Lincoln that the United States should immediately begin the construction of an interoceanic canal across the Isthmus."	**Butler's solution:** "I know of a concession of the United States of Colombia for a tract of thirty miles wide across the Isthmus of Panama for opening a ship canal. The enlistments of negroes have all of them from two to three years to run. Why not send them all down there to dig the canal?"
Number: "[T]o transport to Central America 50,000 freedmen and begin the work"	**Number:** No estimate given
Supplies: "The Government had the transports, the commissary stores, the material of war."	**Supplies:** "We will take our arms with us...[Y]our stores of provisions and supplies clothing will furnish all the rest."
	Immigration: "After we get down there we shall make a humble petition for you to send our wives and children to us."
	Lincoln's response: "There is meat in that suggestion, General Butler; there is meat in that suggestion."

BUTLER'S BOOK (1892)

Date: Between February and March 25, 1865: "A conversation was held between us after the negotiations had at Hampton Roads"... "I [Lincoln] am to go down to City Point shortly."

Lincoln's introduction: "But what shall we do with the negroes after they are free?"

Lincoln's concern: "[W]e have armed and disciplined and who have fought with us, to the amount, I believe some one hundred and fifty thousand men." "If these black soldiers of ours go back to the South I am afraid they will be but little better off with their masters than they were and yet they will be free men I fear a race war and it will be at least a guerilla war"

Colonization: (Lincoln speaking) "I believe that it would be to export them all to some fertile country with a good climate they could have to themselves."

Interlude: "The second day after that I called early in the morning."

Logistics: "I assure you that using all your naval vessels and all the merchant marine fit to cross the seas with safety it will be impossible for you to transport them...half as fast as negro children will be born."

Butler's solution: "The United States wants a ship canal across the Isthmus of Darien at some proper and convenient point. Now I know of a concession made by the United States of Colombia of a strip thirty miles wide across the Isthmus for that purpose. I have the confidence of the negroes. If you will put me in command of them I will take them down there and dig the canal."

Number: "fifty thousand well equipped men"

Supplies: "It will cost the United States nothing but their pay. The clothing that they wear will be otherwise eaten by moths, the arms are of no worth as we have so many of them in excess; the wagons and equipment will otherwise rust out."

Immigration: "After we get ourselves established we will petition Congress under your recommendation to send down to us our wives and children."

Lincoln's response: "There is meat in that, General Butler; there is meat in that."

Taken jointly, the common details present in all three accounts suggest the story is built around an actual event, albeit one viewable only through a troublesome lens. Therein lies the problem with the Butler anecdote. Historians must sift the truth from Butler's embellishments, knowing for certain that a meeting did occur on April 11, 1865. One need not accept every word of the anecdote to find Lincoln's conversational interest in reviving colonization plausible, even probable. Lincoln anguished about the violent state of racial relations for most of his presidency, and it is conceivable that he was "metaphorically 'doing the figures' one more time" at the end of his life, to quote Henry Louis Gates, Jr.[30] Gideon Welles later remarked that the president feared "a war more terrible than that in which we were now engaged," brought on by the oppression of the freedmen in a postwar South. This same recurrent fear turned Lincoln to colonization at many points in his presidency. Welles observed that it prompted Lincoln to include colonization as "an essential part of his emancipation policy" in 1862.[31] According to Mitchell, Lincoln similarly reaffirmed his commitment to colonization after reading about the murder of blacks during the New York draft riots of 1863. Butler may have witnessed comparable sentiments at the 1865 meeting and developed them into a more fanciful rendering of the conversation with the passage of time.

It is worth noting that the most improbable attributes of the proposal appear in Butler's self-depiction. Butler lavished undeserved praise on his military record, overstated his own reputation as a "friend" of the black "race," and named himself as Lincoln's personal choice to lead the Darien expedition before the proposal was even placed on paper. Lincoln, by contrast, patiently received the general's suggestions, remarking only "there is meat in that."

It is also tempting to find fault in Butler's suspiciously visionary claims about the Panama Canal, an engineering feat more closely associated with the decade of his writing than the Civil War. Such scrutiny may be less intuitive than it first appears. In November 1865 Seward posed a query to General Ulysses S. Grant about the possibility of using soldiers to dig a Darien canal. Grant's response, offered in a private note, suggested, "Colored troops could be sent in sufficient numbers to guard the surveying party against hostile Indians and to do all the labor upon land."[32] Could Grant have heard about Butler's conversation, or perhaps even held a similar discussion with Lincoln at City Point in March? Was the suggestion about using the black troops to do the digging a simple coincidence? The answer is unavoidably speculative. However, Grant's answer establishes with certainty that the government was already exploring its options for a canal in 1865, only months after Butler's interview date.

Some historians have discounted the Butler anecdote based on its inconsistency with a speech by Lincoln the same day of the interview in which he endorsed suffrage rights for the "very intelligent" freedmen "and on those who serve our cause as soldiers." Referencing this event, Neely placed the anecdote "at odds with Lincoln's known views." Boritt similarly interpreted Lincoln's "push . . . for limited suffrage" as a sign of his transformation.[33]

The timing of Lincoln's last speech and the Butler meeting would be "profoundly chilling" if accurate, to quote Gates. This simple juxtaposition with suffrage comments makes Butler's testimony more difficult to accept.[34] Yet Fredrickson and Gates have also both suggested that Lincoln's troublesome colonization views may reflect the unresolved aspect of his thoughts on race at the time of his final speech and his assassination three days later. Other evidence besides Butler seems to bear this out, particularly the series of articles penned by Welles for the *Galaxy* magazine in 1877 in which he described colonization and emancipation as "inseparable" in Lincoln's mind. To Gates this observation is "troubling," perhaps even more so than Butler's anecdote. Unlike the general, Welles enjoys a reputation as a strong source among Lincoln biographers, favored for his copious note-taking and high reliability. Considered alongside the suffrage remarks in Lincoln's last speech, colonization may reflect a famous observation by W. E. B. Du Bois, also echoed by Fredrickson and Gates. Lincoln was "big enough to be inconsistent."[35]

Yet inconsistency alone does not preclude the Butler interview. At least one historian, Kevin Gutzman, goes so far as to suggest that Lincoln's "parsimonious parceling out of the suffrage seems at least consistent with, if not actually demonstrative of, a continued wish to colonize."[36] This view is unlikely to find a popular following among many Lincoln biographers, though it may be easier for the scholarly community to accept Lincoln's cautious suffrage advocacy as a sign of his own divided thoughts. Fredrickson cites the voting rights issue as the "strongest evidence" that Lincoln moved beyond colonization and toward racial egalitarianism. Yet Lincoln's final disposition is admittedly "difficult to resolve because of the paucity of evidence bearing on it and because of the fact that Lincoln's thinking about race may have been in flux at the time of his assassination."[37]

Lincoln knew the gravity and complexity of race relations, and this likely manifested itself in his somewhat contradictory policies. Later in his life Welles chastised Lincoln's critics on this account, noting "it is impossible at this day for those who were not participants to conceive the perplexities attending the disposition of the slavery question."[38] In all probability, Butler witnessed a small facet of Lincoln's evolution on race. Overlooking the general's later embellishment of the story, one can easily see the interview as a part of the process by which Lincoln sought an answer to the dominant question at the end of his presidency, the future of race relations in the United States. Cautious, methodical, and contemplative, Lincoln was still developing his beliefs on that question when he crossed paths with General Butler. Confronted with the prospect of racial violence, he likely entertained a quick thought of colonization as he had done many times before and as had been his administration's official policy before the public barely a year prior to that meeting, if not more recently.[39]

It is perhaps not completely idle reflection to note that longstanding colonizationists like the Blairs and, briefly, even Mitchell, took mid-1865 as a chance to start advocating the policy once more, with no new, updated rationale other than a vague sense that the war's end gave them an opportunity to resume work. Mitchell, in fact, had repeatedly urged Lincoln to avoid pushing large-scale colonization projects in earnest until the war's conclusion. More strikingly, Union general Jacob Dolson Cox won election as a Republican to the governorship of Ohio even after prosuffrage abolitionists at Oberlin got him to reveal his hitherto-private plans for mass racial separation within the boundaries of the U.S.

Although such examples cannot ultimately say anything about Lincoln, it is worth observing that Cox's "pragmatic" pessimism for the prospects of peaceful biracial existence in the nation—and his caveats such as a willingness to enfranchise African Americans if the federal government would not execute the scheme—was framed in well-balanced, nuanced terms with which the late president's thinking might well have tallied. It is also intriguing that, even while incurring the predictable Radical disappointment, some commentators praised the sophistication and seriousness of his schemes.[40] In this brief window of intense uncertainty, before the South's and President Johnson's intransigence forced the debate onto the kind of ground with which we more readily associate Reconstruction, colonization arguably still held some appeal for political moderates and in regions where it had always been more popular. With a brief postwar spike in emigration to Liberia from the former Confederacy, moreover, a hypothetical government colonization scheme—though presumably a pared-down, cheap one without congressional support—might have garnered at least some more-than-hypothetical settlers.

Yet the fact remains that we can never know Lincoln's ideas for the future or what would have become of colonization in the second term of the Lincoln administration. Speculation defies the finality that some would attach to Lincoln's views only for the reason that Lincoln himself was deprived of the opportunity to reach that same level of finality.

Chapter 11

Colonization after Emancipation

Lincoln's colonization policies have always been a troublesome part of his legacy for historians to accept and analyze. Fredrickson touched a nerve in 1975 when, citing the Butler anecdote of a "colonization interview" on the eve of Lincoln's assassination, he wondered whether "Lincoln continued to his dying day to deny the possibility of racial harmony in the United States."[1] Historians have spilt hundreds of bottles of ink since that time attempting to prove or disprove the proposition, ever conscious of the moral gravity its answer could entail. The second wave of colonization programs after January 1, 1863, among them the highly developed British Honduras project, has been overlooked thus far, but it is also a part of Lincoln's legacy. It escaped significant attention by accident, quite probably as the feud that consumed it also scattered its records and overshadowed its story. Incorporating it into the existent and well-developed colonization literature is accordingly a challenging and potentially disruptive task.

The British Honduras project's relationship to the "lullaby" thesis of colonization is perhaps its most readily apparent implication. This argument, which holds that Lincoln espoused colonization as a lullaby to make the Emancipation Proclamation politically acceptable, is contradicted by his administration's active attempts to secure and establish colonization sites in the Caribbean well after January 1, 1863. In its typical formulation the lullaby thesis rests on the belief that Lincoln was insincere when he attached colonization to the preliminary Emancipation Proclamation of September 1862 and included it in his address to Congress that December. Rather, he only did so to ease the more radical final proclamation in January. This theory reduces colonization to an auxiliary function in a near-providential drive to the stand-alone policy of emancipation, at most an abandoned stepping-stone in Lincoln's evolution of thought if not an outright ruse. After the proclamation, Lincoln's colonization policy is assumed to have consisted of little more than the administrative fulfillment of the Île à Vache project's obligations and, eventually, the rescue of its survivors in an act of benevolent resolution to a rejected policy. In addition to these requisite assumptions about Lincoln's motives, the lullaby thesis depends upon the absence of colonization records after January 1, 1863.

We find no evidence from the British Honduras colony or any of the lesser Caribbean projects to commend the lullaby thesis. Much to the contrary, they attest to the fault of the argument's basic assumptions by illustrating Lincoln's active pursuit of colonization throughout 1863. Lincoln's actions in the weeks after his New Year's Day announcement reflect a direct continuation of the West Indies "emigration" program he presented to Congress in December 1862, its development only immediately affected by the emancipation policy insofar as it rapidly expanded the population of "contrabands" to recruit. Lincoln's conversations with Lyons and Hodge similarly signify his preoccupation with the southern contrabands intended for colonization by the Americans and desired by British canvassers for their agricultural skills. While irregular at times, Lincoln's pursuit of the policy in British Honduras is also certain and specifically stated. He directly initiated it by way of a dialogue with Lyons in early 1863, and his personal intervention twice revived the negotiations after inaction and hostility from his subordinates over the following summer.

The West Indies programs defy the lullaby thesis on at least one other count. To mollify northern fears of emancipation the conjectured strategy required a clear and public overture toward colonization. Lincoln's December 1862 address to Congress serves this role only when it is also assumed that colonization ceased shortly after the proclamation. The West Indies projects continued for another year, and they were conducted in full secrecy for most of their existence. The diplomatic back channels of their negotiation had the effect of cloaking the effort, partly by design. If the secrecy was intended to palliate an anxious public, the people heard nothing of the scheme between Lincoln's December 1862 address and September 1863, when Mitchell's articles supplied its first substantive details to the press and Menard returned from Belize with reports for the black community. In the interval the British and American governments remained virtually silent. The press took only a passing notice of Hodge's mission upon his arrival; none elaborated on its results; more often, they prematurely dismissed it.[2] The corollary Dutch negotiations were kept even further from public view, confined entirely to the U.S. Legation in The Hague and the halls of the State Department in Washington.

If Lincoln intended these policies to assuage the northern public and prepare it to accept emancipation, he failed spectacularly in communicating this message. The second wave of colonization projects remained sufficiently shrouded that it escaped the attention of Lincoln's own personal secretaries and a century of historians after them. Indeed, hindsight can easily conceal the fact that at the time, the press only picked up on the existence of the Île à Vache expedition in a fragmentary way, too. Most newspapers seem to have become aware of it for the first time with sketchy details of the departure of its ships well into 1863, and additional stories appeared only when reports of neglect and abuse gradually trickled in. What use, then, is a lullaby that is never sung?

This does leave a lingering question as to the significance of Lincoln's removal of colonization and compensated emancipation from the final Emancipation Proclamation, an event which was perhaps more responsible for misdirecting scholars than any other deliberate, self-contained act. It is extremely doubtful that we will ever know what he meant by the omission, and for all that the authors have tried to demonstrate the dangers of putting words into Lincoln's mouth where there is no evidence, it seems fair to say that he was probably too conscientious a man to have accidentally left them out in this case. But historians have always known not to draw sweeping inferences from the ostensible disappearance of compensated emancipation, an offer which Lincoln in fact held out as late as the Hampton Roads conference, when the Confederacy was just two months from defeat. In many ways, this work is the counterpart warning for colonization.

The most obvious conclusion would have to be that while Lincoln still hoped that both of these policies might play a part, emancipation could not *depend* on them. This is a lesson that he would have learned by late 1862 from both the intransigence of the border states regarding gradual, compensated emancipation and the setbacks experienced in pursuing colonization, both abroad and at home, as Congress embarrassingly and blatantly failed to answer the call of his second annual message. Furthermore, Lincoln was always painfully aware that an executive proclamation premised on contestable war powers was at risk of being reversed once the hostilities were over, especially if political opponents came to power. He might have felt that to include in the final version something that could be construed by a later administration, legislature, or judiciary—wrongly, perhaps, but conceivably so in such a gray area—as contractual preconditions to freedom, would jeopardize that greater goal. Paradoxically, it is possible that the more tenuous Lincoln felt his edict to be, the less likely he was to hedge it with qualification and to justify it with allusion to ongoing but hitherto fruitless policies.

But if this does approximate his train of thought, it also reflects the very real possibility that he personally wished to further both compensation and colonization after New Year 1863 as much as he ever had. This argument actually seems even stronger if one accepts that they were *less* linked to each other for Lincoln than they would have been in the minds of earlier generations or those of small 'c' conservative, old-fashioned, gradual emancipationists.[3] If his interest in black emigration was not for public palliation, then this suggests that Lincoln was not merely trying to offer a familiar colonization-compensation package to a certain part of the political spectrum, but rather that he maintained a genuine interest in each. As we have seen, he pursued both on their individual merits at different times and did not consider his options on either cut off by any putative failure to "pull off," in one fell swoop, an overarching policy modeled on the preliminary proclamation of September.

In fact, even Lincoln's conservatism defies such easy labeling to a significant degree. His plans for voluntary emigration lacked the callous deportation to which more serious racial separatists subscribed, while his gentle chiding of some of the public's more lurid concerns about an enlarged free black population provides just the most obvious example of the comparatively benign reasoning to his brand of colonization. In light of all this, Gates wisely urges historians to split up some very basic equations that have long been used to categorize his racial beliefs. "One of the most striking conclusions that a close reading of Lincoln's speeches and writings yielded to me was that "slavery", "race" and "colonization," were quite often three separate issues for him. Sometimes these issues were intertwined in Lincoln's thinking, but far more often they seem to have remained quite distinct, even if we have difficulty in understanding or explaining how this could have been so."[4]

On immediate reflection, this thesis is most obviously applicable to 1850s Lincoln. Eric Foner recently underlined the basic but often overlooked point that Abe's enthusiastic interest in colonization predated his return to politics—let alone such time that he might have the scope to attack slavery—and thus severely strains the lullaby thesis.[5]

Furthermore, Mark E. Neely has recently published a persuasive rebuttal of the "Myth That Lincoln Prepared the People for Emancipation," having sifted through newspaper reports from 1862 to find that the political parties were too entrenched over emancipation for talk of colonization to do anything but preach to the (actually rather lacking) converted. Even sympathizers in principle felt embarrassed at the lack of realism underpinning the president's call for elaborate amendments to engraft colonization and compensation onto the Constitution and responded with an awkward silence.[6] While this does not necessarily preclude political motives from being behind Lincoln's public words on colonization—if one argues instead that he simply misjudged the matter—it still beggars belief that he did not get a sense of this negative reaction in the year between his first and second annual messages. But of course, he almost certainly did: if it says much about Lincoln's beliefs that he continued pursuing negotiations for black resettlement into 1863, it says even more that he did this in private, away from the ridicule of the press and his congressional antagonists. All in all, it would be wise to completely avoid tying Lincoln's thinking on colonization to electoral considerations.

We find greater nuance in the implications of the Caribbean projects to the "change of heart" thesis. Significant as it was to Lincoln and to the country alike for other reasons, the Emancipation Proclamation produced no immediate moral reckoning on colonization for the president. He did not waver from his pursuit of the policy, be it abruptly in January or gradually to round out the early spring. In fact, Lincoln did little to change the course of the "emigration" policy he laid before Congress in December other than to drop his insistence upon a formal Senate-ratified convention at Britain's request. Plans for such a convention, or treaty, with the Netherlands advanced to the final stages of an agreement until Seward withdrew them upon recognizing the improbability of Senate assent.

Lincoln personally left little to indicate a direct role in the failure of these efforts. To the contrary, he rescued them from the same War Department policies that many historians cite as evidence he had changed his mind by the spring's end. Even as black regiments proved themselves in battle at Milliken's Bend and Fort Wagner, he pursued the emigration projects with personal attention and diligence when he handed Hodge a signed authorization to recruit black laborers and when Seward, at Lincoln's prodding, finally acceded to Britain's proclamation of the ports.

Even though the British Honduras colony came closest to fruition, its biggest obstacle was always politics. For reasons known only to them, Mitchell and Usher allowed their personal disdain to impede and ultimately derail the projects. Mitchell made Secretary Usher the scapegoat for his problems and preoccupied himself with wresting the colonization budget from the secretary's tight control. Usher saw the emigration commissioner as a nuisance, best dealt with by inconveniencing rules and exclusion from the department's policy discussions. Britain's internal disputes avoided this level of personal rancor, but politics impeded their contribution to the project too, as the Foreign Office's apprehensiveness clashed with the Colonial Office's enthusiasm for labor.[7]

It remains possible that Lincoln experienced a change of heart on colonization, although at a later date than the current consensus and for reasons having as much to do with political pragmatism as with philosophy. He was a principal driving force behind the British project, and he sustained it through 1863, by personal intervention when necessary. If Lincoln contributed to the scheme's demise it was only by abstention. He abandoned the project only by declining to resuscitate it yet again after the self-destructive actions of his subordinates.

Holding to this assumption, the story of the Mitchell-Usher feud helps to explain the reasons for Lincoln's "change of heart." As Welles and Hay both suggested, Lincoln was constantly frustrated by the corruption and infighting that colonization tended to attract. Mitchell and Usher personified the tendencies of a dysfunctional administrative system. The policy mandate of the Emigration Office completely succumbed to the personal differences of its chief administrator and its cabinet department overseer, many of them petty and trivial. The breakdown of this bureaucracy explains the decline in colonization efforts in 1864 more than any other single reason. New colonization proposals, which had previously flowed into Mitchell's office by the day, ceased entirely. Existing negotiations faltered, consumed by an administrative war of words and paperwork. With Congress already reeling from the Île à Vache fiasco and in need of wartime funds, the feud provided a sufficient pretext to eliminate the colonization budget. Thus if Lincoln backed away from colonization around July 1, 1864, he likely did so from sheer political fatigue.

The last ten months of Lincoln's presidency left the most frugal historical record on colonization. It consists of only two pieces of evidence: Lincoln's petition to Bates over Mitchell's salary, concluded in early January 1865; and the contentious Butler interview of April 11. For reasons discussed and barring new document discoveries, Butler's interview is resolvable only through abstraction. It requires the historian to formulate an informed interpretation based on incomplete information and a factually problematic account that nonetheless appears to be built on an underlying kernel of truth. Still, it is tempting to take the scarcity of colonization evidence in this period as a sign of Lincoln's declining interest.

Two questions emerge from this increasingly conjectural venture. First, does colonization's disappearance from the record signify Lincoln's abandonment of the policy as he moved toward a more egalitarian view of race? His careful though limited endorsement of black suffrage in Louisiana lends credence to an affirmative answer. Alternatively, the sparse paper trail may signify the predictable results of colonization's administrative collapse and repeal by Congress the previous year, where sorting out the Emigration Office's payroll consumed Lincoln's limited time for the policy until the war's end.

This raises the second question. Did Lincoln intend to resume colonization in his second term? Hay's diary entry attributed some finality to Lincoln's "slough[ing] off" in frustration, though hindsight appraisal of the British projects, and Hay's general ignorance of them, illustrates that he was not party to the president's innermost thoughts on this matter. Welles acknowledged a similar frustration but contended that Lincoln "by no means abandoned his policy." Historians must wrestle between the absence of any conclusive rejection of colonization by Lincoln, circumstantial evidence of its decline after 1864, signs of a progressive movement in his beliefs in early 1865, and reminiscences claiming his intent to revive the earlier colonization policy on the eve of his assassination, all written after his passing and most separated from the event by decades. Excepting speculation drawn upon these circumstances, a definitive answer remains elusive.

Still, the volume of evidence provided by the British Honduras project and other Caribbean efforts indicates that most historians have been far too quick to assign closure to Lincoln's colonization program. In the wake of these discoveries, scholars should also ensure that their scrutiny of the fragmentary or potentially biased sources does not become *so* stringent and skeptical as to veer into inconsistency by holding them to standards not applied to other skimpily recorded details which have proven more amenable to the Lincoln canon.

For instance, Bates was personally for black deportation and encouraged the president to continue his emigrationist policies. But in dealing with Mitchell's salary claim he was writing a routine administrative letter and had no incentive to put words in Lincoln's mouth, though admittedly its exact phrasing leaves an ambiguity as to whether he was seriously looking to find some means of continuing the policy now that the money had gone, or just clarifying in a neutral, matter-of-fact way what was theoretically possible with the appropriations repealed. Welles was racially conservative but inveighed against the corruption of schemes like Chiriquí both at the time and in his later articles; it is telling, therefore, that he remembered Lincoln's deep commitment to colonization in an article otherwise striving to rescue his boss's reputation from the emerging commonplace that Seward had been the administration's real statesman. Butler had personal reasons to exaggerate Lincoln's praises for his dubious military record, but little motive to make up a distinctive conversation on race relations, one that he consistently recounted many times. Mitchell was a lifelong believer in the separation of blacks and whites and our only source on some remarks that Lincoln supposedly made to that effect. But we have identified nothing that he committed to print to be untrue, have positively corroborated several details with other sources, and have noticed that he brought to light only three or four reported conversations with Lincoln where he could have fabricated many.

The upshot of the evidence is that colonization remained on the table well beyond the Emancipation Proclamation, and its persistence until the end of Lincoln's presidency ought not to be readily dismissed.

It is this prospect that poses the greatest challenge for Lincoln's reputation in memory as the concept of colonization conveys something repugnant to the modern reader. It strikes at the heart of egalitarianism, holding that different races belong in different climates, theoretically self-governing but separate and apart from each other. This premise carries with it the inference that two races are incapable of cohabiting, save in circumstances where one oppresses the other. The error in this claim is not difficult to recognize. The exact meaning for its historical adherents is.

The prospect that the "Great Emancipator" subscribed to colonizationist beliefs, particularly at the end of his life, seems to completely dispel his popular reputation as a racial egalitarian. From this uneasy query though comes the necessary task of distilling Lincoln the man from Lincoln the legend. If Lincoln died a colonizationist, and such a prospect cannot be conclusively rejected in light of the present evidence, historians may need to reconcile his legacy with Fredrickson's challenge from some three decades ago. Doing so will unavoidably disturb a popular image, though it also opens a new dimension of human complexity to Lincoln's life.

Perhaps colonization's real significance in the 1863–1865 timeframe is its relationship to Lincoln's own evolving personal beliefs on race. When Lincoln embraced colonization he usually expressed it with a benevolent motive, even if retrospection deems this intent misguided. He continuously offered his schemes as a response to the oppression of free blacks and slaves. This is surely a fault of the historical literature, to treat Lincoln's notion of colonization as though it were somehow retrograde *in his own mind,* and therefore destined for the chop in the wake of a personal epiphany after New Year 1863—gradual or otherwise—even as scholars have noted that he publicly presented it as a humane solution to possibly insuperable problems. This error seems all the greater when one considers that, had Lincoln been insincere and wanted to use colonization to pander to racists' concerns, it would have made far more sense to hint that it would be compulsory, and that he would pursue it by means easier than a canvassing campaign for emigrant volunteers, than trying to win virtually unattainable majorities in Congress for relevant constitutional changes.

Ever the experimenter and always the problem solver, Lincoln likely saw colonization as one of many avenues to approach an anguishing difficulty that had no simple resolution. Retrospection correctly deems this program a folly, but to his contemporaries racial politics were a complex and uncharted course. Nor was he alone in this thinking; black abolitionists such as Menard and Garnet saw a possible escape from the United States' racial problems in a colony abroad. To these free black leaders, and perhaps even to Lincoln, colonization presented a voluntary alternative to a future in the United States where the country's commitment to civil rights was anything but certain. This too is no small point: we treat colonization as though it reflected Lincoln's own private views of the worth of African Americans, whereas Butler and Mitchell hint at a recurring concern with the question of whether *other* white Americans could live peacefully alongside blacks. Although this is not to try to rescue Lincoln as a racial progressive—as abolitionists argued, dangling the prospect of colonization justified others' prejudice and helped moderates duck questions of the future shape of America—a distinction may be drawn between personal disdain for African Americans and the kind of pessimistic social outlook which had in fact long been the intellectual mainstay of much of the colonizationist movement.[8]

Historians have tended rather too much to let the cart of "egalitarianism" and other abstract concepts pull the horse of realistic perspective in attempting to comprehend the range and sophistication of human thinking. Lincoln always showed a great propensity for juggling options. He issued a message calling for a gradual, constitutional, and compensated end to slavery—one which we now know to have been much more sincere than is normally accepted—a month shy of his proclamation of immediate freedom for the majority of American slaves. As to specific colonization plans, for a time in late 1862 and early 1863, he was interested in no fewer than three schemes—Chiriquí, Île à Vache, and the British option—simultaneously, though he put more work into one than the others at different points.[9]

On a larger scale but in similar vein, there is nothing to have stopped him feeling some degree of hope for racial integration in the future yet harboring doubts. Lincoln's real but somewhat noncommittal interest in black enfranchisement, which was severely weakened in practice by his unwillingness to force it on a South that he refused to accept as fully out of the Union, is in some ways a good mirror image of a voluntary colonization which had run out of practical outlets by 1865 but which he might well have hoped to revive. Likely neither represented Lincoln's definitive plan for all African Americans, in all places, at all times—and they probably never could do, when even the permanence of emancipation had seemed at risk just the year before. Politically, it made a lot of sense for Lincoln to keep his options open in a fast-changing world in which he was struggling for the middle ground, and this complemented a practical streak in his behavior which was unwilling to gratuitously "hold for naught" any potential course of future action.[10]

Lincoln also approached colonization with characteristic patience as evidenced by his method of trial and adjustment. The British Honduras project repeatedly affirmed these traits. Lincoln turned to it as an answer to the problems he encountered in 1862. The BHC, backed in its venture by the sanction of Her Majesty's Government, presented a reliable business partner in an enterprise that otherwise attracted swindlers, speculators, and petty tyrants. Britain's strength resolved a problem encountered in the Chiriquí project, where political instability in the Colombian government reinforced doubts about the validity of the proposed colony's land grant. The use of emigration canvassers comported well with Lincoln's insistence upon voluntary colonization. Furthermore, the scheme's design itself represented a shift in Lincoln's thought on the mechanics of executing his colonization program. For reasons both political and administrative, he eventually abandoned the original strategy of contracting colonization to private firms selected from a multitude of solicitations seeking a portion of the colonization fund. In its place, he sought and obtained a simple agreement with a crown-backed company and with minimal cost to the U.S. government.

The difficulty in resolving Lincoln's final position on colonization may simply indicate the continuation of his thought process, his tinkering, and his contemplative reflection on an exceedingly complex and paradoxical issue. If his views on race were still evolving, or even revolving, at the time of his death they cannot be expected to satisfy a rigid demand for consistency or an unrealistic desire for conclusiveness. Like his presidency, they ended unfinished, an accident beyond his control or the country's wishes. That circumstance merits neither the disparagement nor the wishful veneer that some have hastily attached to Lincoln's colonization record. It is fact that Lincoln pursued colonization as policy. But his pursuit of that policy fluctuated, veering off in directions he never anticipated and leaving its intended final disposition known only to him.

Notes

CHAPTER 1
THE CURIOUS POLITICS OF COLONIZATION

1. John Nicolay and John Hay, *Abraham Lincoln: A History* (New York: The Century Co., 1890), 6:355.

2. See "Eulogy on Henry Clay" and "Outline for Speech to the Colonization Society," in Roy P. Basler et al., eds., *Collected Works of Abraham Lincoln,* 9 vols. (New Brunswick, NJ: Rutgers University Press, 1953–1955), 2:121–32, 298–99.

3. "Speech at Springfield, June 26, 1857" in Basler et al., eds., *Collected Works,* 2:121–32, 298–99, 409.

4. "Fourth Debate with Stephen A. Douglas at Charleston, Illinois," in Basler et al., eds., *Collected Works,* 3:145–6.

5. Elisha O. Crosby and Charles A. Barker, *Memoirs of Elisha O. Crosby,* (San Marino, CA: The Huntington Library, 1945), 87.

6. "Annual Message to Congress, December 3, 1861," in Basler et al., eds., *Collected Works,* 5:48.

7. James Mitchell to Lincoln, July 1 and July 3, 1862, Abraham Lincoln Papers, Library of Congress.

8. "Appeal to the Border State Representatives to Favor Compensated Emancipation" and "Preliminary Emancipation Proclamation," in Basler et al., eds., *Collected Works,* 5:317–19, 434.

9. See Paul J. Scheips, "Lincoln and the Chiriqui Colonization Project," *Journal of Negro History* 37 (1952): 418–53; Charles A. Wesley, "Lincoln's Plan for Colonizing Emancipated Negroes," *Journal of Negro History* 6 (1919): 7–21; James D. Lockett, "Abraham Lincoln and Colonization: An Episode That Ends in Tragedy at L'Ile a Vache, Haiti, 1863–1864," *Journal of Black Studies* 21 (1991): 428–44.

10. Nicolay and Hay, *Lincoln: A History,* 6:357. Henry J. Raymond, *The Life and Public Services of Abraham Lincoln,* (New York: Derby and Miller Publishers, 1865), 509.

11. Robert Penn Warren. *The Legacy of the Civil War: Meditations on the Centennial.* (New York: Random House, 1961), 59–60.

12. Allen Thorndike Rice, ed., *Reminiscences of Abraham Lincoln by Distinguished Men of His Time* (New York: North American Publishing, 1886), 61.

13. John Niven, *Gideon Welles: Lincoln's Secretary of the Navy* (Baton Rouge:

Louisiana State University Press, 1994), 570; Gideon Welles, "Administration of Abraham Lincoln," *Galaxy* 24, no. 4 (1877).

14. Phillip Shaw Paludan, "Lincoln and Colonization: Policy or Propaganda?" *Journal of the Abraham Lincoln Association* 25 (2004), 34.

15. Michael Vorenberg, "Abraham Lincoln and the Politics of Black Colonization," *Journal of the Abraham Lincoln Association* 14 (1993), 42. For another example of this view see Matthew Pinsker, *Lincoln's Sanctuary* (Oxford: Oxford University Press, 2005), 95.

16. Eric Foner, *Our Lincoln: New Perspectives on Lincoln and His World* (New York: W.W. Norton, 2008), 161, 163. Stephen Oates and Mark E. Neely have similarly traced the transformation of Lincoln's colonization policy to the Emancipation Proclamation. See Oates, *With Malice toward None: The Life of Abraham Lincoln* (New York: Harper & Row, 1977), 341–42; Neely, *The Abraham Lincoln Encyclopedia* (Columbus, OH: McGraw-Hill, 1981), 83.

17. Foner, *Our Lincoln,* 165, 166.

18. Paludan, "Lincoln and Colonization," 35–36; Benjamin Quarles, *Lincoln and the Negro* (New York: Da Capo Press, 1991), 193; Mark E. Neely, Jr. "Lincoln and Race," in Brian Lamb and Susan Swain, eds., *Abraham Lincoln: Great American Historians on Our Sixteenth President* (New York: Public Affairs, 2008), 211.

19. George M. Fredrickson, *Big Enough to Be Inconsistent: Abraham Lincoln Confronts Slavery and Race* (Cambridge, MA: Harvard University Press, 2008), 110–11.

20. James M. McPherson, *Ordeal By Fire: The Civil War and Reconstruction* (New York: A.A. Knopf, 1982), 277; Gabor Boritt, *The Lincoln Enigma* (Oxford: Oxford University Press, 2002), 13–14.

21. McPherson's argument was made in a scathing review of Michael Lind's recent biography, which interpreted Lincoln's colonizationist statements as being sincere. See Lind *What Lincoln Believed* (New York: Doubleday, 2005). The review prompted a heated exchange of letters between Lind and McPherson in which the latter strongly reiterated the lullaby thesis. James M. McPherson, "What Did He Really Think about Race?" *New York Review of Books,* 54–55, March 29, 2007; McPherson, "Letters: Lincoln & Race," *New York Review of Books,* 54–57, April 26, 2007. A recent essay by Mark E. Neely Jr. has questioned whether Lincoln's August 14, 1862, colonization address was an intended palliative for emancipation, though this interpretation remains a minority viewpoint. See Neely, "Colonization and the Myth that Lincoln Prepared the People for Emancipation," in William A. Blair and Karen Fisher Young, eds., *Lincoln's Proclamation: Emancipation Reconsidered* (Chapel Hill: University of North Carolina Press, 2009), 45–74. In contrast, Michael Burlingame recently attributed the 1862 push for colonization to congressional pressures and an attempt to assuage border state slaveholders. See Burlingame, *Abraham Lincoln: A Life* (Baltimore: Johns Hopkins University Press, 2009), chapter 28.

22. Abraham Lincoln. "Address on Colonization to a Deputation of Negroes," in Basler et al., eds., *Collected Works,* 5:370–75.

23. Fredrickson, *Big Enough to Be Inconsistent,* 113–14. Foner, *Our Lincoln,* 162–63. A similar take may also be found in Manisha Sinha's argument that "Lincoln's

eventual abandonment of colonization after he decided to free the slaves was a triumph of abolitionism, particularly black abolitionism." See Sinha, "Allies for Emancipation? Lincoln and Black Abolitionists," in Foner, ed., *Our Lincoln,* 185.

24. Phillip W. Magness, "Benjamin Butler's Colonization Testimony Reevaluated," *Journal of the Abraham Lincoln Association* 29–1 (2008): 1–28.

25. The authors have opted to use the naming conventions of the historical time period for purposes of consistency with the relevant historical documents and colonial records. British Honduras, British Guiana, and Surinam (occasionally called Dutch Guiana) correspond, respectively, to the modern nations of Belize, Guyana, and Suriname.

26. Nicolay and Hay, *Lincoln: A History,* 6:357. Frederic Bancroft took notice of preliminary colonization negotiations with Britain but concluded "Lord Russell declined the proposition" and limited his discussion to the better-known projects in Haiti and Panama. *The Life of William H. Seward.* (New York: Harper & Brothers Publishers, 1900), 2:347. William Archibald Dunning remarked that "a like privilege was granted to the British Honduras Company" to recruit free black emigrants for agricultural purposes, but concludes like Hay and Nicolay that Lincoln only "made two distinct efforts to settle negroes outside of the United States." *Studies in Southern History and Politics* (New York: Columbia University Press, 1914), 16–17. Charles H. Wesley acknowledges that the government received proposals from British Honduras and Guiana to allow the recruitment of emigrants from northern port cities but notes little more of the project. "Lincoln's Plan for Colonizing Emancipated Negroes," *Journal of Negro History* 6 (1919): 15–16. Thomas Schoonover includes the two British colonies among a list of locations where "preliminary terms" were considered but ultimately abandoned due to a "collapse in negotiations" over the matter of citizenship for the freedmen. "Napoleon Is Coming! Maximilian Is Coming?" in Robert E. May, ed., *The Union, the Confederacy, and the Atlantic Rim* (West Lafayette, IN: Purdue University Press, 1995), 115. Kinley L. Brauer includes a similar list of proposals but concludes they failed as "Seward was unresponsive." "The Slavery Problem in the Diplomacy of the Civil War," in Michael Krenn, ed., *Race and U.S. Foreign Policy from the Colonial Period to the Present: A Collection of Essays.* (Levittown, PA: Garland Publishing, Inc., 1998), 454.

27. In 1947 Luveta Gresham gave the British Honduras proposal its first acknowledgment beyond Hay and Nicolay's list by noting that colonial agents from British Honduras had submitted a proposed contract for the site to the Interior Department in early 1863. Limited in access to only a partial accounting of the project though, Gresham erroneously concluded that "the President still withheld his consent." See Gresham, "Colonization Proposals for Free Negroes and Contrabands during the Civil War," *Journal of Negro Education* 16 (1947): 31. A decade later, Tinsley Lee Spraggins repeated this mistake, concluding that the Secretary of the Interior "rejected the applications of the planters of British Guiana and British Honduras" for emigrants. See Spraggins, "Economic Aspects of Negro Colonization during the Civil War," Ph.D. Diss. (Washington, D.C.:

American University, 1957), 197–98. More recently, Gerald Horne's 2007 history of the slave trade in South America recounted preliminary details of the proposal as well but concluded that the "scheme passed into stillbirth." See Horne, *The Deepest South: The United States, Brazil, and the African Slave Trade* (New York: New York University Press, 2007), 181–82. Eric Foner is the most recent historian to spot evidence of the British Honduras project but reckoned, also mistakenly, that the colonial agents abandoned their pursuit after encountering opposition from the War Department. See Foner, *Our Lincoln,* 161–62.

28. Among the secondary literature, only a colonial history of Belize by Wayne Clegern and a prior study of Lincoln's colonization policies by one of the authors of this volume have acknowledged the developments of the British Honduras settlement beyond the spring of 1863. Both present the project as ancillary material to other historical discussions. A very brief discussion of the proposed Surinam treaty appears in Robert F. Durden's biography of James Shepherd Pike, the U.S. minister to the Netherlands under Lincoln. See Wayne M. Clegern, *British Honduras: Colonial Dead End, 1859–1900* (Baton Rouge, LA: Louisiana State University Press, 1967) 20–35; Magness, "Butler's Colonization Testimony," 15–18; Durden, *James Shepherd Pike: Republicanism and the American Negro, 1850–1882* (Durham, NC: Duke University Press, 1957), 86–90.

CHAPTER 2
AMERICAN FREEDMEN, BRITISH LABOR

1. James Mitchell, *Brief on Emigration and Colonization* (Washington, D.C.: M. Polkinhorn & Son, 1865), 10; Abraham Lincoln, "Commission of Emigration Agency," August 4, 1862, National Archives and Records Administration of the United States (hereafter cited as NARA), "Records of the United States Department of the Interior, African Slave Trade and Negro Colonization, Records of 1854–1872," RG 48, M 160.

2. Mary Edward Mitchell, *Memoirs of James Mitchell: Statesman, Educator, Minister* (Mt. Zion, GA: Mt. Zion Seminary, 1905, reprinted 1939), 6-9.

3. James Mitchell (interview), "Lincoln and the Negro," *St. Louis Daily Globe-Democrat,* August 26, 1894.

4. *Ibid.*

5. "To William H. Seward," in Roy P. Basler et al., eds., *Collected Works of Abraham Lincoln,* 9 vols. (New Brunswick, N.J.: Rutgers University Press, 1953–1955), 4:547.

6. Mitchell, *Brief on Emigration and Colonization,* 7; Lincoln, "Commission of Emigration Agency," August 4, 1862, Slave Trade and Colonization Records; Roy P. Basler (*Collected Works*, 5:375 note 1) notes that Mitchell's first appearance in the Interior Department records dates to May 28, 1862. Other documents suggest an earlier arrival. Caleb Smith suggested to Lincoln that Mitchell be given charge of his department's colonization activities a few weeks prior to that date, and Mitchell

published his first report on the subject through the Government Printing Office on May 18. See Smith to Lincoln, May 5, 1862, and Mitchell, "Letter on the Relations of the White and African Races," Abraham Lincoln Papers, Library of Congress. He may have been in Washington prior to May 1862 though. Mitchell stated in an 1894 interview that he witnessed a conversation with Lincoln about the Trent Affair on December 20, 1861 (*St. Louis Daily Globe-Democrat,* August 26, 1894). Mitchell's later writings are characterized by an uncommon ability to supply specific dates many years after an event. Mitchell is known to have kept an extensive personal diary, now lost and last seen in the possession of his niece who used it to compose a short biography in the early twentieth century. See M.E. Mitchell, *Memoirs of James Mitchell.*

7. *St. Louis Daily Globe-Democrat,* August 26, 1894. Mitchell attributed the same response to Lincoln in an 1865 colonization pamphlet. See Mitchell, *Brief on Emigration and Colonization,* 11.

8. No. 39, Eyre to Newcastle, July 5, 1862, in *Correspondence Respecting Emigration from the United States to the West Indies,* (London: Colonial Office, June 19, 1863), in National Archives of the United Kingdom, Colonial Office Records (hereafter cited as CO) 884/2, 1-2. This publication is hereafter cited as *Correspondence Respecting Emigration.*

9. No. 81, Eyre to Newcastle, September 20, 1861, in *Correspondence Respecting Emigration,* 2; No. 512, Newcastle to Eyre, October 31, 1862, in *Correspondence Respecting Emigration,* 3-4.

10. No. 203, September 4, 1862, in James J. Barnes and Patience M. Barnes, *The American Civil War through British Eyes* (Kent, OH: Kent State University Press, 2005) 2:168-69.

11. Francis B. Carpenter, *Six Months at the White House with Abraham Lincoln* (1866; reprint, Lincoln: University of Nebraska Press, 1995), 291. It is noteworthy that Seward's secretary George E. Baker made a similar observation in a private letter from June 1865, writing that "Lincoln and Seward never disagreed but in one subject – that was the colonization of the negroes." See Gaillard Hunt, *Israel, Elihu and Cadwallader Washburn: A Chapter in American Biography* (New York: Macmillan, 1925), 116.

12. No. 203, September 4, 1862, in Barnes and Barnes, *American Civil War,* 2:168-69.

13. No. 225, September 15, 1862, in Barnes and Barnes, *American Civil War,* 2:175-76.

14. September 26, 1862, in Gideon Welles, *The Diary of Gideon Welles* (New York: W. W. Norton, 1960), 1:152-53.

15. Edward Bates, Howard K. Beale, ed. *The Diary of Edward Bates, 1859-1866.* (Washington, D.C.: Government Printing Office, 1933), 262-64.

16. No. 254, September 28, 1862, in Barnes and Barnes, *American Civil War,* 2:189-90.

17. No. 255, September 28, 1862, in Barnes and Barnes, *American Civil War,* 2:190.

18. "England and American Slavery," *Douglass' Monthly,* excerpted from the *London Morning Star,* March, 1863.

19. Gideon Welles later wrote that colonization and emancipation were "indispensably and indissolubly connected" in Lincoln's mind. See Gideon Welles, "Administration of Abraham Lincoln," *Galaxy* 24, no. 4 (1877): 439. Mitchell (*St. Louis Daily Globe-Democrat,* August 26, 1894) made a similar claim, describing the January 1, 1863, proclamation as a continuation of the colonization projects initiated along with the preliminary proclamation the previous September.

20. Seward to Adams, September 30, 1862, reproduced in *Correspondence Respecting Emigration,* 31-32.

21. No. 512, Newcastle to Eyre, October 31, 1862, in *Correspondence Respecting Emigration*, 4.

22. O. Nigel Bolland, *Colonialism and Resistance in Belize* (Kingston, Jamaica: Cubola Productions, a division of University of the West Indies Press, 2003), 156-58.

23. Monica Schuler, *"Alas, Alas, Kongo": A Social History of Indentured African Immigration into Jamaica, 1841-1865* (Baltimore, MD: Johns Hopkins University Press, 1980), 7-8, 29; Rosanne M. Adderley, *"New Negroes from Africa": Slave Trade Abolition and Free African Settlement in the Nineteenth Century Caribbean* (Bloomington, IN: Indiana University Press, 2006), 74-75.

24. "Our Belize Correspondence," *New York Herald,* June 23, 1860.

25. *ATTORNEY GENERAL BRITISH HONDURAS v. JOHN HODGE*: Petition to the Privy Council by John Hodge of Belize and also of No 2 Great Saint Helens in the City of London, Merchant, August 8, 1863, TS 25/1273; Cardwell to Eyre, No. 97, January 3, 1865, in Offices: Council, CO 123/118.

26. Janet L. Coryell, "The Lincoln Colony: Aaron Columbus Burr's Proposed Colonization of British Honduras." *Civil War History,* 43-1:5-16; James Mitchell, *Report on Colonization and Emigration* (Washington, D.C.: Government Printing Office, 1862), 19; No. 134, Seymour to Eyre, December 14, 1862, in *Correspondence Respecting Emigration,* 8-9.

27. "An Act to encourage the immigration of agricultural and other laborers into the colony of British Honduras," Enclosure of Lyons to Seward, June 17, 1863, in *Papers Relating to Foreign Affairs, Accompanying the Annual Message of the President* (Washington, D.C.: Government Printing Office, 1864) 583-4; Hodge to Rogers, November 18, 1862, in *Correspondence Respecting Emigration,* 65; See also Hodge to Rogers, August 23, 1862, in CO 318/237.

28. No. 126, Seymour to Eyre, October 15, 1862, in *Correspondence Respecting Emigration,* 7; No. 134, Seymour to Eyre, December 14, 1862, in *Correspondence Respecting Emigration,* 8-9; No. 101, Eyre to Newcastle, October 24, 1862, in *Correspondence Respecting Emigration,* 7.

29. Alan H. Adamson, "The Reconstruction of Plantation Labor after Emancipation: the Case of British Guiana," in Adamson, Stanley L. Engerman, and Eugene Genovese, *Race and Slavery in the Western Hemisphere: Quantitative Studies* (Princeton, NJ: Princeton University Press, 1975) 457-73; Anthony Trollope, *The West Indies and the Spanish Main* (London: Chapman & Hall, 1860) 163.

30. No. 159, Hincks to Newcastle, August 22, 1862, in *Correspondence Respecting Emigration,* 13-15; No. 12, Edwards to Seward, August 25, 1862, in NARA, "Despatches from U.S. Consuls in Georgetown, Demerara, British Guiana," General Records of the Department of State, RG 59, T 336. It is worth noting that Edwards's praise for the colony in his official correspondence carries the caveat of his desire to maintain strong political relations with the colonial government. As he noted to Seward in a confidential letter at the same time, "If Mr. Walker knew that I wrote any thing unfavorable to this colony in that dispatch – it might make me unpopular here and I could not be of so much service to the Government." See Edwards to Seward, Private and Confidential, August 25, 1862, in William Henry Seward Papers, University of Rochester, Microform Edition, Reel 71.

31. No. 256, Stuart to Russell, September 29, 1862, in Barnes and Barnes, *American Civil War,* 2:191.

32. Walker to Stuart, September 30, 1862, in *Correspondence Respecting Emigration,* 29. During his visit Walker also presented his colony to an audience of free blacks, who reacted coldly to the scheme and lodged their grievances with the harsh colonial labor system of Demerara. See "The Colored People of Brooklyn upon the Proclamation and the Colonization of the Contrabands," *New York Times,* October 3, 1862.

33. Walker to Lyons, November 8, 1862, in National Archives of the United Kingdom, Foreign Office Records (hereafter cited as FO), 115/332; Mitchell to Lyons, February 28, 1863 in FO 115/392; Circular Dispatches from the Secretary of State; Newcastle to the Governors of Jamaica, British Guiana, and Trinidad, October 16 and November 21, 1862, in *Correspondence Respecting Emigration,* 19; Elliot to Hammond, October 14, 1862, in *Correspondence Respecting Emigration,* 51.

34. No. 169, Russell to Stuart, October 24, 1862, in *Correspondence Respecting Emigration,* 30; Hammond to Rogers, October 29, 1862, in *Correspondence Respecting Emigration,* 30; Russell to Stuart, October 30, 1862, in *Correspondence Respecting Emigration,* 31; Russell to Stuart, October 4, 1862, in Russell's personal papers, National Archives of the United Kingdom, Public Records Office (hereafter cited as PRO), 30/22/96.

35. No. 253, Adams to Seward, October 30, 1862, in *Papers Relating to Foreign Affairs, Accompanying the Annual Message of the President* (Washington, D.C., Government Printing Office, 1862), 228.

36. Hodge to Rogers, November 18, 1862, in *Correspondence Respecting Emigration,* 65; Rogers to Hodge, November 29, 1862, in *Correspondence Respecting Emigration,* 66; Rogers to Hammond, November 21, 1862, in *Correspondence Respecting Emigration,* 53-54; Hammond to Rogers, November 24, 1862, in *Correspondence Respecting Emigration,* 32-33, 37. Hammond to Rogers, September 24, 1862, in CO 318/235.

38. No. 546, Lyons to Russell, December 26, 1862, in Barnes and Barnes, *American Civil War,* 2:277-81.

39. *Ibid.*, Rogers to Hodge, January 16, 1863, in *Correspondence Respecting Emigration,* 66-67.

CHAPTER 3
MR. LINCOLN'S HOBBY

1. James J. Barnes and Patience P. Barnes, *Private and Confidential: Letters from British Ministers in Washington to the Foreign Secretaries in London, 1844-67* (Selinsgrove, PA: Susquehanna University Press, 1993), 313.

2. Abraham Lincoln, "Annual Message to Congress," December 1, 1862, in Basler et al., eds., *Collected Works,* 5:520.

3. Noah Brooks, Michael Burlingame, ed., *Lincoln Observed: Civil War Dispatches of Noah Brooks* (Baltimore, MD: Johns Hopkins University Press, 2002), 48.

4. Charles Tuckerman, an investor in the Île à Vache project, suggested many years later that Lincoln had difficulty in convincing his subordinates to finalize this contract, even in its early stages. After several government delays owing to rumors put forth by "opponents of the scheme," Tuckerman traveled to Washington in the spring of 1863 to confer with Lincoln and Usher about finalizing a stalled portion of the contract. Much to Lincoln's irritation, the secretary of the interior missed the scheduled meeting. After waiting for over an hour Lincoln then reportedly turned to Tuckerman, stating "you've had enough trouble about it, and so have I." He then affixed his signature, stating "I guess it's all right" and transmitted the order to the Interior Department. See Charles K. Tuckerman. "Personal Recollections of Abraham Lincoln," *Magazine of American History* (May 1888), 19:413.

5. Barnes and Barnes, *Private and Confidential,* 315; No. 69, January 23, 1863, in James J. Barnes and Patience M. Barnes, *The American Civil War through British Eyes,* (Kent, OH: Kent State University Press, 2005), 2:305. Lincoln himself reportedly referred to colonization as his "hobby" in a conversation with Senator Charles Sumner in 1862. See Charles Edwards Lester. *The Life and Public Services of Charles Sumner* (New York: United States Publishing Company, 1874), 386.

6. Barnes and Barnes, *Private and Confidential,* 313.

7. Mitchell to Nicolay, January 26, 1863, in Abraham Lincoln Papers, Library of Congress. This paper has been misfiled in 1862 due to legibility problems with the document's date. January 26 corresponds to the designated "Monday morning" of 1863 though.

8. No. 78, January 27, 1863, in Barnes and Barnes, *American Civil War,* 2:306-8.

9. *Ibid.*

10. Receipt of Thomas S. Malcom, February 6, 1863, Slave Trade and Colonization Records.

11. No. 145, Lyons to Russell, February 10, 1863, in Barnes and Barnes, *American Civil War,* 2:328.

12. No. 177, Lyons to Russell, February 24, 1863, in Barnes and Barnes, *American Civil War,* 3:7.

13. Foreign Office Memorandum, February 19, 1863, Slave Trade and Colonization Records.

14. Usher to Seward, March 2, 1862, in *Senate Executive Documents,* No. 55, Serial 1238, 39th Congress, 1st Session, 23-24.

15. No. 214, Lyons to Russell, March 10, 1863, in Barnes and Barnes, *American Civil War,* 3:20-21.

16. No. 10, Leas to Seward, February 15, 1863 in NARA, "Despatches from U.S. Consuls in Belize, British Honduras," General Records of the Department of State, RG 59, T 334. There is some evidence that Leas's letters influenced the slow progression of the U.S. policy on British Honduras. Seward forwarded copies of the despatch to Usher for review. See Usher to Seward, September 21, 1863 in *Executive Documents,* No. 55, Serial 1238, 39th Congress, 1st Session, 34.

17. Benjamin Moran, Appointment Secretary for the U.S. Legation in London, to Seward, March 29, 1863, Slave Trade and Colonization Records. See also W.H. Ward to Lincoln, March 27, 1863, Lincoln Papers, Library of Congress.

18. No. 19, Leas to Seward, March 17, 1863, Despatches from U.S. Consuls in Belize.

19. "A Home for the Colored Man." *New York Evening Post,* September 8, 1851; William W. Anderson, *A Description and History of the Island of Jamaica* (Kingston: George Henderson, 1851); William W. Anderson, "The British West Indies," *National Era,* October 25, 1849. Anderson migrated to Jamaica from Scotland in 1833, shortly before the British emancipation policy took effect in the West Indies colonies. He served as a member of the colonial assembly and a solicitor of the court for Kingston. Anderson represented Jamaica in the British and Foreign Anti-Slavery Society, dating at least to 1840 if not earlier. In 1844 Anderson entered into a business partnership with longtime friend George William Gordon, the noted Jamaican abolitionist and anticolonialist. Not long after his involvement in the BHC scheme, Anderson unsuccessfully petitioned Lieutenant Governor Eyre to stay his notorious execution warrant for Gordon, who was accused of inciting the Morant Bay Rebellion of 1865.

20. C. Peter Ripley, ed. *The Black Abolitionist Papers* (Chapel Hill: University of North Carolina Press, 1986), 2:154-55, 164; William Wemyss Anderson, "The British West Indies," *National Era*, October 25, 1849.

21. "From Washington," *Chicago Tribune*, April 25, 1863; *Savannah Daily Morning News,* March 12, 1863; "Summary of News from the Federal States," *Richmond Record of News, History and Literature,* July 2, 1863; "Honduras and Hayti," *The African Repository* (Washington, D.C.: William H. Moore), 39:344.

22. No. 361, Lyons to Russell, April 27, 1863, FO 5/934; Hodge to Lyons, July 9, 1863, CO 318/239.

23. Hodge to Lyons, July 9, 1863, CO 318/239.

24. No. 361, Lyons to Russell, April 27, 1863, FO 5/934.

25. Hodge to Usher, May 6, 1863, Slave Trade and Colonization Records; *Emigration and Colonization: Proposals for the Establishment of Townships of Colored People in British Honduras, Central America* (London and Belize: British Honduras Company, 1863); Hodge to Usher, May 14, 1863, enclosed in Hodge to Lyons, July 9, 1863, CO 318/239.

26. Hodge to Howe, April 29, 1863, James Morrison MacKye Papers, Library of Congress.

27. Mackie to Owen, May 13, 1863. Records, 1862-1864, American Freedmen's Inquiry Commission, MS Am 702 (110), Houghton Library, Harvard University, Cambridge Massachusetts.

28. "Emigration and Colonization" and "Lecture," *Christian Recorder,* May 23, 1863; "Lecture," *Christian Recorder,* May 30, 1863.

29. "A Meeting at the Shiloh Church," *Douglass' Monthly,* June 1863.

30. Joan R. Sherman, ed., *African-American Poetry in the Nineteenth Century* (Champaign: University of Illinois Press, 1992), 282. In 1863 Menard authored a widely published response to Frederick Douglass after the latter condemned colonization: "Sir, the inherent principle of the *white majority* of this nation is to refuse FOREVER republican equality to the black minority. A government, then, founded upon heterogeneous masses in North America would prove destructive to the best interest of the white and black races within its limits" (J.W.M. [John Willis Menard], "A Reply to Frederick Douglass, by a Colored Man," *Douglass' Monthly,* April 1863); Some of Menard's early poems also emphasized colonizationist topics: "LIBERIA! O immortal name! / To Africa's sons and daughters; / It glows like an undying flame, / Upon their hearts and altars!" (John Willis Menard. "Liberia," *The Christian Recorder,* March 7, 1863).

31. See Menard to Usher, April 11, 1863, Slave Trade and Colonization Records.

32. Dickson to Lyons, May 11, 1863, FO 115/393; Lyons to Dickson, May 12, 1863, FO115/397; Lyons to Dickson, 21 May 1863, 115/397.

33. Hodge to Usher, May 6, 1863, and May 7, 1863, Slave Trade and Colonization Records.

34. Hodge to Lyons, July 9, 1863, CO 318/239; John Hodge, "Memorandum on Self Sustaining Emigration," May 9, 1863, Slave Trade and Colonization Records.

35. Lyons to Russell, April 27, 1863, FO 5/934; Hodge to Lyons, July 9, 1863, CO 318/239.

36. Usher to Hodge, May 11, 1863, enclosed in Hodge to Lyons, July 9, 1863, CO 318/239. See also the revised version appearing in *Senate Executive Documents,* No. 55, Serial 1238, 39th Congress, 1st Session, 32.

37. Evidence of Stanton's involvement is indicated in the letters of Assistant Secretary of War P. H. Watson to Usher, May 12, 1863, and Whiting to Watson, May 13, 1863, Slave Trade and Colonization Records.

38. "Memorandum," Hodge to Seward, May 11, 1863, in Seward Papers, Reel 185.

39. Hodge to Usher, May 14, 1863, Slave Trade and Colonization Records; Lyons to Eyre, June 18, 1863, FO 5/934.

40. "Colonization of the Blacks," *New York Times,* May 17, 1863. Eric Foner (*Our Lincoln,* 162) is one of the few recent historians to take any notice of Hodge's mission, but he concluded, based upon the *Times*'s mistaken report, that the project ended without any result in May. Hodge remained in the United States until July though after seeing a renewal of interest.

41. Montgomery Blair. *Comments on the Policy Inaugurated by the President, in a Letter and Two Speeches* (New York, NY: Hall, Clayton, and Medole Printers, 1863), 10.

42. *Ibid.,* 12.

43. Charles A. Dana, *Recollections of the Civil War* (Lincoln: University of Nebraska Press), 170-71.

44. Hodge to Lyons, July 9, 1863, CO 318/239. Hodge does not identify either Mitchell or Blair by name in his report to Lyons, though he states that he "was strongly urged to apply direct to the President who alone possessed the supreme power and had the entire control of the contrabands, and who desired my success." The unnamed cabinet official who volunteered to help him is undoubtedly Blair, who provided Hodge with an introductory note for a meeting with Lincoln. See Blair to Lincoln, June 12, 1863, Lincoln Papers, Library of Congress; and Phillip W. Magness, "Benjamin Butler's Colonization Testimony Reevaluated" *Journal of the Abraham Lincoln Association* 29-1 (2008), note 62.

45. The meeting probably occurred shortly after Usher's May 11 rejection of the proposal. Hodge referenced it in a letter to Mitchell about "carrying out your and Mr. Blair's desire." See Hodge to Mitchell, October 25, 1863, Slave Trade and Colonization Records.

46. Mitchell to William H. Seward, May 19, 1863, private; Mitchell to Frederick W. Seward, May 20, 1863, in Seward Papers, Reel 78.

47. Usher to Hodge, June 10, 1863, in *Senate Executive Documents,* No. 55, Serial 1238, 39th Congress, 1st Session, 33.

48. Hodge to Lyons, July 9, 1863, CO 318/239.

49. See Magness, "Butler's Colonization Testimony," note 61 regarding this document. Existent versions include (1) a secretary's "copy" in the Department of Interior files (Slave Trade and Colonization Records), misdated as 1862, (2) a published transcription of the order with correct dates in an 1865 pamphlet (Mitchell, *Brief on Emigration and Colonization*, 15), and (3) the copy provided to the British Legation in Washington (FO 115/394). The final disposition of an original in Lincoln's pen remains a puzzle for historians. Lincoln appears to have signed two copies, which were placed in the possession of Hodge and Mitchell. Hodge displayed the original bearing Lincoln's signature to Lyons but only deposited the surviving copy at the legation. He was allowed to retain the original and likely departed for Belize with the document in hand. Mitchell's original, which presumably bears a disapproving inscription from Stanton, was returned "to my own files." An October 1863 letter from an Interior Department clerk states that Mitchell has a letter "from the President covering the whole Colonization scheme" in his files (Thompson to Whiting, October 21, 1863, Slave Trade and Colonization Records). If existent, this document likely remained in Mitchell's possession until his death in 1903, and papers were dispersed among his heirs.

50. *Ibid.,* Hodge to Lyons, July 9, 1863, CO 318/239. Like many facets of the BHC project, Lincoln's signature of approval has received scant notice from historians, most of whom prematurely concluded that Lincoln "withheld his consent" as per Luveta Gresham, "Colonization Proposals for Free Negroes and Contrabands during the Civil War," *Journal of Negro Education* 16 (1947). Michael Vorenberg first discovered Lincoln's signature while researching the Emigration Office records, though he did not associate it with Hodge's mission, little known at the time

beyond Gresham's brief description. Absent this connection to the extensive diplomacy that produced the document, Vorenberg actually downplays Lincoln's signature as a "private" concession and suggests it is evidence of his waning colonization interests. See "Abraham Lincoln and the Politics of Black Colonization," *Journal of the Abraham Lincoln Association* 14 (1993), note 37.

51. James Mitchell (interview), "Lincoln and the Negro," *St. Louis Daily Globe-Democrat,* August 26, 1894.

52. Hodge to Lyons, June 13, 1863 as enclosed in Russell to Lyons, No. 567, June 19, 1863, FO 5/934.

CHAPTER 4
THE CONTRABANDS QUESTION

1. Lyons was personally supportive of Hodge's work and outwardly expressed a desire for its success. He privately doubted whether the Americans would carry through though, as he wrote to Acting Governor Eyre in Jamaica. "I am not so sanguine about its success, as are Mr. Hodge and Mr. Dickson, and I must observe that it is by no means certain that the government of the United States will consistently persevere in promoting or even in permitting the emigration of coloured people from this country" (Lyons to Eyre, June 18, 1863, in FO 5/934). Lyons to Russell, June 19, 1863, in James J. Barnes and Patience P. Barnes, *Private and Confidential: Letters from British Ministers in Washington to the Foreign Secretaries in London, 1844-67* (Selinsgrove, PA: Susquehanna University Press, 1993), 325; Hodge to Lyons, June 16, 1863, enclosed in Russell to Lyons, No. 567, June 19, 1863, in FO 5/934; No. 567, Lyons to Russell, June 19, 1863 in James J. Barnes and Patience M. Barnes, *The American Civil War through British Eyes* (Kent, OH: Kent State University Press, 2005), 3: 69-70. Lyons to Seward, June 17, 1863, in *Papers Relating to Foreign Affairs, Accompanying the Annual Message of the President* (Washington, D.C.: Government Printing Office, 1864), 582-83.

2. Barnes and Barnes, *Private and Confidential,* 326; Lyons to Russell, June 19, 1863, in Barnes and Barnes, *American Civil War,* 3:69-70; Foreign Office to Colonial Office, "Draft" July 9, 1863, FO 5/934.

3. Elliot to Layard, July 31, 1863, FO 5/934; Hodge to Lyons, July 3, 1863, enclosed in Lyons to Russell, No. 663, July 20, 1863, FO 5/934. See also CO 318/239.

4. Hodge to Lyons, July 9, 1863, CO 318/239.

5. Elliot to Layard, July 31, 1863, FO 5/934.

6. *Ibid.*

7. Foreign Office to Lyons, No. 437, "draft," August 5, 1863, FO 5/934. Russell received word of Hodge's return to Belize shortly after acceding to Newcastle's arguments on the contrabands issue. He interpreted Hodge's departure as a sign that the recruitment effort was suspended for the time being. See Foreign Office to Colonial Office, "draft" August 8, 1863, FO 5/934.

8. Seward to Lyons, August 10, 1863, in *Papers Relating to Foreign Affairs (1864),* 620.

9. James Mitchell (interview), "Lincoln and the Negro," *St. Louis Daily Globe-Democrat,* August 26, 1894. Mitchell's reminiscence is removed from the event by almost three decades and should be afforded appropriate scrutiny, but the conversation is lent some credibility given Seward's belated reply to Lyons the same week and Mitchell's newspaper articles, written the next day. Lincoln's reputed note to Seward has not been identified. The Brown University library possesses a brief memorandum from Lincoln to Seward dated August 10, 1863, reading "I have for a good while had this particular question under consideration; and my judgment that the within, substantially, should be the answer to Lord Lyons." Unfortunately, the referenced attachment has long since been lost. Roy Basler speculated that the attachment pertained to Navy Department affairs with the British Admiralty, as discussed in another letter from Lincoln to Gideon Welles on July 25. See Roy P. Basler et al., eds., *Collected Works of Abraham Lincoln,* 9 vols. (New Brunswick, NJ: Rutgers University Press, 1953–1955), 6:378-80. Given the date's coincidence with Seward's answer to Lyons, it is entirely possible that the lost attachment is that referred to by Mitchell, though confirmation will remain elusive barring its rediscovery.

10. James Mitchell. "The Colored People of the United States," *Methodist,* August 19, 1863, in Slave Trade and Colonization Records; Mitchell, "Negro Emigration and Colonization," *New York Observer,* September 10, 1863.

11. Mitchell to F. W. Seward, September 15, 1863, in NARA, "Miscellaneous Letters of the Department of State," RG 59, M179, Reel 204.

12. Edith Menard, "John Willis Menard: First Negro Elected to the U.S. Congress, First Negro to Speak in the U.S. Congress," *Negro History Bulletin,* 27, no. 3 (1964):53-54.

CHAPTER 5
THIS MOST DESIRABLE COUNTRY

1. Charles Babcock, *British Honduras, Central America: A Plain Statement to the Colored People of the U.S. Who Contemplate Emigration,* (Salem, MA: C. Babcock, 1863), 1. The *Antonio Mathe* was named after the proprietor of a merchant firm in British Honduras and made the regular mail run between New York and Belize City for over a decade. She participated in the wood trade from the colony until wrecking on a reef in 1865.

2. Hodge informed Lyons that he invited the delegation in anticipation of the contrabands issue being resolved. "For this purpose I take with me delegates from the northern and western states of this country, and from Canada also . . ." Hodge to Lyons, July 9, 1863, CO 318/239.

3. Leas, No. 60, August 20, 1863, Despatches from U.S. Consuls in Belize.

4. "Emigration to Honduras," *Liberator,* March 24, 1864.

5. See J. W. Menard, Charles Babcock, C. F. Key, P. Stafford, G. Washington, and W. A. Lovelette, "To the Department of the Interior," Slave Trade and Colonization Records.

6. "West India Correspondence," *The Anti-Slavery Reporter and Aborigines' Friend,* January 1, 1864

7. Enclosure by Leas on August 10, 1863, Despatches from U.S. Consuls in Belize.

8. Babcock, *British Honduras,* 4–5.

9. Babcock, *British Honduras,* 6–8; J.B. Hyde to Rogers, September 26, 1863, CO 318/239.

10. Babcock, *British Honduras,*12–13, 9; No. 10, Leas to Seward, February 15, 1863, Despatches from U.S. Consuls in Belize.

11. Babcock, *British Honduras,* 15.

12. John Alder Burdon, *Archives of British Honduras* (London: Sifton Praed & Co, Ltd, 1935), 3:254.

13. "West India Correspondence," *Anti-Slavery Reporter.*

14. G. L. C., "John Willis Menard, Esq.," *Christian Recorder,* September 26, 1863. The Philadelphia-published *Christian Recorder* was affiliated with the African Methodist Episcopal Church. The newspaper frequently aligned with Garnet's organization and printed notices from the African Civilization Society.

15. "Meeting at the Shiloh Church," *Douglass' Monthly,* June 1863.

16. Junius C. Morel, "Brooklyn Correspondence," *Christian Recorder,* August 1, 1863.

17. Junius C. Morel, "Brooklyn Correspondence," *Christian Recorder,* October 10, 1863; "From Junius," *Christian Recorder,* October 17, 1863.

18. "Supplement to the Constitution of the African Civilization Society," *Christian Recorder,* January 2, 1864.

19. John Floyd Miller, *The Search for a Black Nationality: Black Emigration and Colonization, 1787–1863* (Urbana: University of Illinois Press, 1975), 260–63; "Grand Emancipation—Celebration of the Emancipation of the National Capital," *Liberator,* May 8, 1863.

20. "The African Civilization Society," *Christian Recorder,* November 14, 1863. A subsequent report referenced the society's support for emigration policies and noted they are "now struggling to do good to the contrabands in the South, and also doing all they can to forward the good work in Africa, Central and South America, and British West Indies" (Junius C. Morel, "Brooklyn Correspondence," *Christian Recorder,* October 24, 1863).

21. Menard to Lincoln, September 16, 1863, Slave Trade and Colonization Records.

22. In addition to Menard's letter, a British newspaper recorded that Menard "furnished President Lincoln with an able report of British Honduras" ("Washington, from an occasional correspondent," *Anglo-American Times,* January 2, 1869). Menard's lost report was also referenced in a brief biographical sketch by one of his descendants. "Menard was accordingly commissioned and proceeded to Balize [*sic*]

where he was officially received by the Governor. The investigation was made and his report was subsequently published. However, nothing further was ever done" (E. Menard, "John Willis Menard," 53).

23. "Estella, in Honduras, 1863" in J. Willis Menard, *Lays in Summer Lands* (Washington: Enterprise Publishing Company, 1879), 11.

24. Babcock, *British Honduras,* 16 (emphasis original); *Liberator,* March 24, 1864.

25. Charles Leas, "Belize or British Honduras" (unpublished manuscript, 1863), chapter 6, in Despatches from U.S. Consuls in Belize.

26. No. 81, Leas to Seward, October 25, 1863, Despatches from U.S. Consuls in Belize. The relationship between Leas and Hodge appears to have benefited from an incident in September when the *New York Herald* published a scurrilous allegation about mismanagement in the Belize City consular office. In response, Hodge organized a petition of the colony's leading citizens attesting to Leas's character. See Hodge et al. to Seward, October 6, 1863, Despatches from U.S. Consuls in Belize.

27. Hodge to Mitchell, October 27, 1863, Slave Trade and Colonization Records.

28. Heriot to Lord Stanley of Alderley, Postmaster General, October 20, 1863, copy, CO 123/114.

29. No. 81, Leas to Seward, October 25, 1863, and Hodge to Leas, October 25, 1863, Despatches from U.S. Consuls in Belize.

30. Hodge to Mitchell, October 27, 1863, Slave Trade and Colonization Records. In the letter Hodge mentions only recently learning that "Earl Russell had instructed Lord Lyons to sanction the hiring of Contrabands for this colony."

31. *Ibid.*

32. Leas to Seward, "Document 2," October 25, 1863, Despatches from U.S. Consuls in Belize; Hodge to Mitchell, October 27, 1863, Slave Trade and Colonization Records.

33. Hodge to Leas, October 25, 1863, Despatches from U.S. Consuls in Belize.

34. Mitchell to Hodge, November 24, 1863, Slave Trade and Colonization Records.

35. Seward to Usher, October 19, 1863, Seward Papers, Reel 137.

36. Burdon, *Archives of British Honduras,* 3:254. This December 13 "prohibition" presents one of the greatest remaining mysteries of British Honduras's participation in the emigration project. It was not reported in any of the routine Colonial Office correspondence. Government records from Belize were extremely irregular in this period, and no copies of the *Government Gazette* for December 1863 survived in the British National Archives. The prohibition order is known only through a single logged entry for this date in the 1935 record book of British Honduras's public archives by Burdon, then serving as governor of the colony, and an equally brief mention by Seymour in his 1864 address to the colonial legislature.

37. No. 117, Leas to Seward, January 21, 1864, Despatches from U.S. Consuls in Belize.

38. K.O. Laurence, *Immigration into the West Indies in the Nineteenth Century,* (Barbados: Caribbean University Press, 1971), 30–37.

39. *Ibid.*, 24–25; James Rodway, *A History of British Guiana* (Georgetown, British Guiana: 1894), 3:107.

40. Eyre to Cardwell, No. 61, May 6, 1864, and Eyre to Cardwell, No. 62, May 23, 1864, CO 123/115; "Anglican Neglect in Honduras and West Indies." *The Colonial Church Chronicle, Missionary Journal, and Foreign Ecclesiastical Reporter* (London: Rivingtons, Waterloo Place, 1865), 222:481.

41. Hyde to Newcastle, September 26, 1863, CO 318/239.

42. See Donald C. Simmons, *Confederate Settlements in British Honduras* (Jefferson, NC: McFarland, 2001).

43. No. 131, Leas to Seward, March 10, 1864, Despatches from U.S. Consuls in Belize.

44. Robertson to Rogers, April 30, 1864, CO 123/118.

45. Eyre to Cardwell, No. 95, August 24, 1864, CO 123/117.

46. Robertson to Rogers (annotation), April 30, 1864, CO123/118.

CHAPTER 6
A SELF-SUPPORTING SCHEME

1. Hincks to Newcastle, No. 159, August 22, 1862, in *Correspondence Respecting Emigration from the United States to the West Indies* (London: Colonial Office, June 19, 1863), 13–15.

2. Elliot to Hammond, September 24, 1862, with enclosure of copy of Hincks to Walker, August 23, 1862, FO 5/934.

3. Hincks to Newcastle, No. 159, August 22, 1862, in *Correspondence Respecting Emigration,* 14.

4. Alan H. Adamson, "The Reconstruction of Plantation Labor after Emancipation: the Case of British Guiana," in Adamson, Stanley L. Engerman, and Eugene Genovese, *Race and Slavery in the Western Hemisphere: Quantitative Studies* (Princeton, NJ: Princeton University Press, 1975), 460–68.

5. Hincks to Newcastle, No. 184, November 18, 1863, CO 111/342.

6. Murdoch to Rogers, December 28, 1863, CO 386/95.

7. Hincks to Newcastle, No. 170, November 2, 1863, CO 111/342.

8. Murdoch to Rogers, December 28, 1863, CO 386/95.

9. London *Times,* December 19, 1863.

10. Murdoch to Rogers, December 28, 1863, CO 386/95.

11. "British Guiana: License for the Conveyance of Immigrants on Bounty from the Ports of Philadelphia, New York and Boston to the Colony of British Guiana," Miscellaneous Letters of the Department of State, NARA, RG 59, M 179, Reel 213.

12. Murdoch to Rogers, June 1, 1864, CO 318/243.

13. Murdoch to Rogers, April 8, 1864, and Murdoch to Rogers, July 30 1864, CO 386/96. This removal of consuls from the business of emigration was still current and apparently settled in Walcott to Elliot, August 29, 1865, CO 386/96.

14. Murdoch to Rogers, April 8, 1864, CO 386/96.

15. Murdoch to Rogers, July 30, 1864, CO 386/96.

16. Murray to Rogers, July 9, 1864, enclosing Archibald to Murray, June 29, 1864, CO 318/243.

17. Hincks to Newcastle, No. 171, November 2, 1863; No. 174, November 7, 1863; No. 184, November 18, 1863, CO 111/342.

18. London *Times,* August 4, 1863.

19. The secretive departure of the Vache expedition and the British minister's ensuing request for information in themselves belie the idea that colonization was an openly publicized sop to racists. This likely had much to do with the very open reporting of some of the problems which had bedeviled the Chiriquí project the previous fall, and with the embarrassment and apathy with which Lincoln's calls for congressional assistance to colonization had been met. See Lyons to Archibald, No. 178, July 18, 1863, FO 115/386.

20. Archibald to Thompson, February 29, 1860; January 17, 1861; September 29, 1865, Ambrose W. Thompson Papers, Library of Congress.

21. Hammond to Rogers, February 25, 1865, enclosing Burnley to Russell, No. 88, February 3, 1865, and in turn enclosing Carlisle to Burnley, January 28, 1865, copy, CO 318/245.

22. Walcott to Elliot, August 29, 1865, CO 386/96; Murdoch to Rogers, May 28, 1866, CO 318/246; Carnarvon to Grant, No 3, July 18, 1866, CO 124/11.

CHAPTER 7
SECRETARY SEWARD AND THE DUTCH TREATY

1. Robert F. Durden, *James Shepherd Pike: Republicanism and the American Negro, 1850–1882* (Durham, NC: Duke University Press, 1957), 87.

2. The authors wish to point out that they do not know Dutch and have not attempted to research the topic in the archives of the Netherlands. The files of the National Archives suggest that the Dutch Legation in Washington was involved only in the initial approach, though, which probably rules out the existence of the kind of evidence left by Hodge and Lyons, external observers who were given privileged access to the inside of government and then reported the developments that they witnessed there to another party.

3. Roest Van Limburg to William H. Seward, July 19, 1862, in NARA, "Notes from the Dutch Legation," RG 59, T 5.

4. Seward to Van Limburg, July 22, 1862, "Notes to Foreign Legations in the United States from the Department of State: the Netherlands," NARA, RG 59, M 99, Reel 75.

5. James S. Pike to William H. Seward, No. 91, June 26, 1863, in NARA, "Despatches from United States Ministers in the Netherlands," RG 59, M 42, Reel T 23.

6. Durden, *James Shepherd Pike,* 89; enclosures with Pike to Seward, No. 91, June 26, 1863, Despatches from United States Ministers in the Netherlands.

7. Seward to Pike, No. 113, July 31, 1863, in NARA, "Diplomatic Instructions of the Department of State: the Netherlands," RG 59, M 77, Reel 123.

8. Pike to Seward, No. 103, October 8, 1863, Despatches from United States Ministers in the Netherlands.

9. Pike to Paul Van der Maesen de Sombreff, November 17, 1863, in NARA, "Records of Foreign Service Posts: Diplomatic Posts: the Netherlands," RG 84, the Netherlands, Vol. 79.

10. Pike to Seward, No. 113, December 16, 1863, Despatches from United States Ministers in the Netherlands.

11. David Hunter Miller, *Treaties and Other International Acts of the United States of America* (Washington, D.C.: Government Printing Office, 1948), 8:856–857.

12. Pike to Seward, No. 114, December 19, 1863, Despatches from United States Ministers in the Netherlands.

13. James S. Pike, *First Blows of the Civil War: The Ten Years of Preliminary Conflict in the United States from 1850–1860* (New York: The American News Company, 1879), 162–64.

14. Pike to William P. Fessenden, January 13, 1863, James Shepherd Pike Papers, 1849–1869, Library of Congress.

15. Pike to Fessenden, April 6, 1864, Pike Papers, Library of Congress.

16. Durden, *James Shepherd Pike*, 93.

17. Seward to Pike, No. 142, February 15, 1864, Diplomatic Instructions of the Department of State: The Netherlands.

18. Van Limburg to Seward, February 9, 1864, Notes from the Dutch Legation; Seward to Van Limburg, February 12, 1864, Notes to Foreign Legations in the United States from the Department of State: The Netherlands.

19. Pike to Seward, No. 125, March 16, 1864, Despatches from United States Ministers in the Netherlands.

20. Henry Sawyer to Frederick W. Seward, No. 106, January 27, 1864, in NARA, "Records of Foreign Service Posts: Consular Posts: Paramaribo," RG 84, Paramaribo, Vol. 12.

21. L. Marx to William H. Seward, May 16, 1864, in NARA, "Miscellaneous Letters of the Department of State," RG 59, M 179, Reel 212.

22. Seward to Pike, No. 113, July 31, 1863, Diplomatic Instructions of the Department of State: The Netherlands.

23. Durden, *James Shepherd Pike*, 93.

24. Jay Sexton, *Debtor Diplomacy: Finance and American Foreign Relations in the Civil War Era, 1837–1873* (Oxford, Oxford University Press, 2005), chapters 3–4.

25. Pike to Seward, No. 55, June 23, 1862, Despatches from United States Ministers in the Netherlands.

26. For emancipation in Surinam, see Pieter Emmer, *"Between Slavery and Freedom: Apprenticeship in Suriname (Dutch Guiana), 1863–73," Slavery and Abolition* (London: F. Cass, 1993), 87–113; Cornelius C. Goslinga, *A Short History of the Netherlands Antilles and Surinam* (Boston: M. Nijhoff, 1979), 156–59;

Pieter Emmer, *The Dutch in the Atlantic Economy, 1580–1880: Trade, Slavery and Emancipation* (Brookfield, VT: Ashgate, 1998), 154–70.

27. Sawyer to Seward, No. 61, September 15, 1862; No. 66, October 25, 1862; No. 74, February 7, 1863; No. 76, March 16, 1863, "Records of Foreign Service Posts: Consular Posts: Paramaribo," RG 84, No. 12.

28. Francis B. Carpenter, *Six Months at the White House with Abraham Lincoln* (1866; reprint, Lincoln: University of Nebraska Press, 1995), 291.

CHAPTER 8
ADMINISTRATIVE DYSFUNCTION, CONGRESSIONAL DISPLEASURE

1. Abraham Lincoln, "Commission of Emigration Agency," August 4, 1862; Smith, "Salary," December 1, 1862 (enclosure of Mitchell to Usher, January 21, 1864), Slave Trade and Colonization Records.

2. Caleb Smith to Mitchell, October 3, 1862, Slave Trade and Colonization Records. Little is known about Augustus A. Smith aside from his appearance as a clerk in the Emigration Office papers. He was appointed by Mitchell with Caleb Smith's sanction on December 26, 1862, and received a salary of $100. See A. Smith to Usher, January 21, 1863, Slave Trade and Colonization Records. Menard was hired around this time as well, his name appearing on Emigration Office letterhead in April 1863. Over the next year he received $110 cumulative in compensation. Prior to his employment at a clerk, Menard obtained funding from the Emigration Office to pay his passage on a fact-finding mission to Liberia with the American Colonization Society. See John P. Usher, "Report of the Secretary of the Interior to the President of the United States pertaining to the transportation, settlement, and colonization of persons of the African race," submitted March 11, 1864, enclosed in *Senate Executive Documents,* No. 55, Serial 1238, 39th Congress, 1st Session, 3-5 (hereafter cited as Usher, "Report of the Secretary of the Interior").

3. Gabor Boritt, *The Lincoln Enigma* (Oxford: Oxford University Press, 2002), 9. Caleb Smith knew Mitchell from prior colonization work in Indiana and strongly favored his appointment to lead the Emigration Office. He wrote Lincoln that "Rev. J. Mitchel [*sic*] is as well qualified for such a service as any person with whom I am acquainted and I think his appointment would be proper and judicious." Smith to Lincoln, May 5, 1862, in Lincoln Papers, Library of Congress. Smith came to Mitchell's defense during the feud with Usher and believed Mitchell's position to be justified under the powers he had approved for the Emigration Office at its creation. Smith to Mitchell, December 22, 1862, Slave Trade and Colonization Records. Mitchell also managed to garner the sympathy of James Harlan, Usher's slated successor, who took office shortly after Lincoln's assassination in 1865. See Harlan to Lincoln, December 31, 1864, in Lincoln Papers, Library of Congress.

4. There is some evidence that the antipathy between Mitchell and Usher traced back to an older political dispute in Indiana, and Mitchell often implied as much.

Their relationship was cool although not overtly hostile at the beginning of Usher's cabinet tenure. Menard appears to have known that Mitchell carried less sway with Usher than with his predecessor and indicated as much in a letter to the Interior Department's chief clerk George Whiting, who was said to "have more influence with Cabinet Officers." See Menard to Whiting, April 23, 1863, Slave Trade and Colonization Records.

5. See Mitchell to Lyons, February 28, 1863, FO 115/392; Lyons to Mitchell, February 28, 1863, FO 115/397.

6. Usher to Lincoln, May 18, 1863, in Lincoln Papers, Library of Congress. Lincoln's copy is a refined version of a heavily edited draft in the Interior Department's files. The draft places a stronger emphasis on the War Department's need of the contrabands, possibly indicating that it was subject to Stanton's suggestions as with Usher's May 11 reply to Hodge, Slave Trade and Colonization Records.

7. For an example see Usher to B. T. Brown, November 3, 1863, in *Senate Executive Documents,* No. 55, Serial 1238, 39th Congress, 1st Session, 38.

8. Whiting to Thompson, October 21, 1863; Mitchell to Usher, October 22, 1863, and Mitchell to Usher, February 3, 1864, Slave Trade and Colonization Records.

9. Whiting to Thompson, October 21, 1863, Slave Trade and Colonization Records. Mitchell transmitted Hodge's October 27 letter to Lincoln on November 25, requesting absolute secrecy. He withheld all updates about the British project from Usher until the following February. "I cannot permit any part of Mr. Hodge's letter to go to the public now – and were it not for the demand you have made for any correspondence…I would not give this letter at this time, but as it may be necessary to justify the position the President has taken in drawing England to our side, I have concluded to let it go" (Mitchell to Usher, February 4, 1864, Slave Trade and Colonization Records).

10. Usher to Mitchell, October 21, 1863, in *Senate Executive Documents,* No. 55, Serial 1238, 39th Congress, 1st Session, 38.

11. Mitchell to Usher, October 22, 1863, Slave Trade and Colonization Records.

12. Smith to Mitchell, December 22, 1863, enclosed in Mitchell to Harlan, June 6, 1865, Slave Trade and Colonization Records.

13. James Mitchell, letter to Methodist clergy, 1863, in Matthew Simpson Papers, Library of Congress.

14. *Ibid.* Rep. Orth's bill created a new cabinet-level "Department of Industry" to oversee freedmen's affairs, among other things. The bill reorganized Mitchell's agency into a "Colonization Bureau" under this department and charged it with the administration of the fund. See H.R. 216, 38th Congress, 1st Session.

15. A secretarial note on the margin of the society's petition to Lincoln nonetheless designated it a "colonization" request.

16. Mitchell to Wilson, October 5, 1863, Lincoln Papers, Library of Congress; Quarles, *Lincoln and the Negro,* 114-15.

17. LeVere et al. to Mitchell, September 12, 1863; Hoadley et al. to Mitchell, September 18, 1863, Slave Trade and Colonization Records. It is probable that

Menard also helped to arrange the meeting and may have opened the society's communication with Mitchell. After returning from Belize in mid-September he spent time in New York with Garnet.

18. LeVere et al., "Address to the President of the United States" November 5, 1863; "Draft Order" in the handwriting of James Mitchell, November 5, 1863. Lincoln Papers, Library of Congress.

19. "The President and the African Civilization Society," *New York Times,* November 13, 1863. A correspondent of the *Christian Recorder* described a speech in late 1863 when "The President of the Society, Rev. G.W. LeVere, presided, and gave an interesting account of the visit which several gentlemen, officers of the society, had made to Washington, and of their highly satisfactory interview with President Lincoln," January 9, 1864.

20. James Mitchell, *Brief on Emigration and Colonization* (Washington, D.C.: M. Polkinhorn & Son, 1865), 17.

21. Usher, "Report of the Secretary of the Interior"; Mitchell, *Brief on Emigration and Colonization*, 12.

22. Abraham Lincoln, "Commission of Emigration Agency," August 4, 1862, Slave Trade and Colonization Records.

23. Wade to Lincoln and Lincoln to Usher, January 18, 1864; Mitchell to Usher, January 21, 1864, enclosing excerpts of Usher to Mitchell, January 20, 1864, Slave Trade and Colonization Records.

24. Disbursement sheet for the Emigration Office and accompanying note of John P. Usher, January 23, 1864, Slave Trade and Colonization Records. It is illuminating to contrast Usher's stringent control of Mitchell's budget requests with the expenses of Senator Samuel Pomeroy, who also conducted his work out of the colonization fund. Pomeroy was entrusted with a $25,000 advance from this fund in late 1862. Over the next two years Usher permitted him to spend the money with little if any oversight, save for providing a final unitemized total to Congress in 1864. Pomeroy's use of the fund became a source for allegations of corruption against him, particularly after the Île à Vache colony fell through.

25. Mitchell to Usher, February 3, 1864, Slave Trade and Colonization Records. Mitchell left a receipt for "papers relating to colonization of Blacks" with the president's office on January 29, 1864, Lincoln Papers, Library of Congress. They do not appear to have been returned.

26. Usher to Mitchell, February 2, 1864, in *Senate Executive Documents,* No. 55, Serial 1238, 39th Congress, 1st Session, 45.

27. Usher to Mitchell, February 3, 1864, in *Senate Executive Documents,* No. 55, Serial 1238, 39th Congress, 1st Session, 46-47.

28. Mitchell to Usher, enclosed "P.S.," and attached correspondence with Hodge, February 4, 1864, Slave Trade and Colonization Records.

29. Lincoln, "To the Senate" in Roy P. Basler et al., eds., *Collected Works of Abraham Lincoln*, 9 vols. (New Brunswick, NJ: Rutgers University Press, 1953–1955) 7:241.

30. Usher, "Report of the Secretary of the Interior."

31. Seward answered with reference to his August 10 memorandum to Lyons. "I

was directed by the President to reply that this government interposes no objection to the voluntary emigration of persons of the class described, and of course none to the proclamation proposed." (Seward to Usher, October 19, 1863. Seward Papers, Reel 137).

32. Ibid. See also accompanying documents in *Senate Executive Documents,* No. 55, Serial 1238, 39th Congress, 1st Session.

33. *Congressional Globe*, 38th Congress, 1st Session, 1274.

34. *Ibid.*, 2218.

35. *Journal of the Senate*, 38th Congress, 1st Session, Wednesday, June 22, 1864, 611.

36. Mitchell to Lincoln, June 1864, Lincoln Papers, Library of Congress. On June 25 Senator Lane of Kansas stated "Yesterday or the day before the Senator from Kentucky renewed his resolution asking for a report of the commissioner of emigration, which has not been answered." Mitchell's letter to the Senate is reprinted in the *Congressional Globe* along with Lane's remarks, 38th Congress, 1st Session, 3261.

37. Usher to Lincoln, June 29, 1864, Lincoln Papers, Library of Congress. After receiving Usher's June 29 letter, a White House secretary attached it to a brief memorandum to the Senate, stating "all the official information possessed by the Department [of the Interior] on the subject of colonization has already been communicated." See "To the Senate," June 29, 1864, Lincoln Papers, Library of Congress. Lincoln endorsed the cover memorandum but never sent it to the Senate. See Basler et al., eds., *Collected Works*, 7:417, note 1.

38. Mitchell to Lincoln, June 1864, Lincoln Papers, Library of Congress. Lincoln's papers only contain Mitchell's cover letter in which he briefly describes its contents and relays complaints about Usher. A revised and amended answer to the Senate resolution was submitted by Mitchell on November 24, 1864. The November report likely mirrors Mitchell's statement to Lincoln in June, excepting an addendum to reflect Congress's repeal of the colonization fund. Mitchell, *Brief on Emigration and Colonization,* 9-14. The cover letter to the report directs Lincoln's attention "to the correspondence of Messrs Hodge and Rolls, relating to Honduras, and the Claims of the British Colonies." These documents were apparently submitted to Lincoln but have since been lost. "Rolls" is John Roles, the British Honduras planter who accompanied Menard's delegation on their visit to the colony's agricultural region. According to the report (Mitchell, *Brief on Emigration and Colonization,* 10-11), his letter contained evidence of an "instance" in which the "military authority" was "impeding the man of color in the execution of his right to emigrate."

39. For example, see Eric Foner, *Our Lincoln: New Perspectives on Lincoln and His World* (New York, NY: W. W. Norton, 2008), 164. It is worth noting that Lincoln continued to press forward on the British projects even after word of the Vache colony's problems reached Washington. In July 1863 Lyons received word from the British consul in Cuba about the "disastrous" voyage of the first ship carrying settlers to the island. He sought to learn more from the administration but

found "the subject is so painful to those of the authorities here who were parties to making the contract, and especially to the President himself, who sanctioned it from motives of benevolence to these unfortunate people, that there is a great reluctance to give any definite information concerning it." Lincoln nonetheless pressed through to finalize the port proclamations agreement a little under a month later. See Lyons to Archibald, No. 178, July 18, 1863, FO 115/386.

40. *Congressional Globe*, 38th Congress, 1st Session, 3261.

41. *Ibid.*, 3261-63.

42. Michael Burlingame and John R. Ettlinger, eds., *Inside Lincoln's White House: The Complete Civil War Diary of John Hay* (Carbondale: Southern Illinois University Press, 1999), 217. For an extended discussion of Hay's diary entry see Magness, "Butler's Colonization Testimony," 11-13.

43. Lincoln had a peculiar habit of being unforthcoming at times about his colonization work, even among allies. Mitchell later recalled that he only learned of the Chiriquí contract in 1862 when a finished copy arrived at his desk. Lincoln similarly bypassed most of his cabinet on the British negotiations of 1863 save for Seward, who was dragged in reluctantly, and Blair, who inserted himself on Hodge's behalf. Discussions of colonization at cabinet meetings were infrequent after September 1862, even as work on the Chiriquí, Île à Vache, and the West Indies projects continued. Perhaps Lincoln saw political prudence in silence, knowing the discord colonization caused.

44. *Diary of John Hay,* 217. This simple explanation for Lincoln's "slough[ing] off" of colonization finds some additional support in an anecdote by Charles Tuckerman about a meeting with Lincoln to discuss the Île à Vache contract in mid 1863. Opponents of colonization had seized upon Kock's reputation as a swindler to stall additional government commitments on the project. Lincoln reportedly confided to Tuckerman that he had become "fully convinced of the baseless character" of Kock. Notwithstanding this realization, the president "assured me he still had the enterprise greatly at heart, and that 'it should go on'" under the supervision of Tuckerman and another investor, Paul S. Forbes. See Charles K. Tuckerman, "President Lincoln and Colonization," *The Magazine of American History,* October 1886, 41.

45. "An Act for the Collection of Direct Taxes in Insurrectionary Districts within the United States, and for Other Purposes," approved June 7, 1862, in *The Statutes at Large, Treaties, and Proclamations of the United States of America* (Boston: Little, Brown and Company, 1863) 12, chapter 98, section 12. One fourth of the proceeds were to be used for colonization.

CHAPTER 9
THE INDEFATIGABLE JAMES MITCHELL

1. James Mitchell, *Brief on Emigration and Colonization* (Washington, D.C.: M. Polkinhorn & Son, 1865), 11, 14.

2. *Ibid.*, 13.

3. The Senate discussed Mitchell's anticipated report, and one member read his letter into the record, promising its delivery in time for the December session of Congress. James Nesmith of Oregon pointed out a potential legal problem with the legislation's wording. "I ask whether the repeal of the appropriation would not necessarily repeal the commissioner and prevent him making a report." James Lane suggested adding language to clarify Mitchell's role after the repeal of the colonization fund, but the debate concluded before the issue could be resolved (*Congressional Globe*, 38th Congress, 1st Session, 3262).

4. Usher served as a Whig member of the Indiana Legislature from 1850 to 1851 while Mitchell directed colonization policy for the state's Democratic governor, Joseph A. Wright. Usher was later an unsuccessful Republican candidate for Congress in 1856, and he served as the state attorney general between November 1861 and March 1862 when he joined the Interior Department as an assistant secretary.

5. Mitchell to Lincoln, September 2, 1864, Lincoln Papers, Library of Congress. Ambrose W. Thompson was the proprietor of the Chiriquí contract of 1862. An envelope endorsement in Lincoln's pen indicates that he read Mitchell's letter. Mitchell made little elaboration about the nature of his past quarrels. Fisher was a proslavery pamphleteer based in Cincinnati who clashed with factions of the Indiana Democratic Party during the 1850s, including, possibly, Mitchell during the latter's involvement with the administration of Governor Joseph A. Wright.

6. Mitchell to Simpson, October 31, 1864, Simpson Papers, Library of Congress.

7. Robert Donald Clark, *The Life of Matthew Simpson* (New York: Macmillan, 1956), 229.

8. Johnson Brigham, *James Harlan* (Iowa City: State Historical Society of Iowa, 1913), 206-7.

9. James Harlan to John Puvey[?], June 7, 1865, John Palmer Usher Papers, Kansas State Historical Society, Topeka; Harlan to Simpson, August 17, 1865, Simpson Papers, Library of Congress.

10. Referencing Smith's December 22, 1863, letter in which the former secretary of the interior encouraged him to appeal to Lincoln for intervention, Mitchell wrote, "I did not show the above to Mr. Lincoln until the fall of 1864 when I made it part of my communication intended for the At. General" (Mitchell to Harlan, June 6, 1865, Slave Trade and Colonization Records).

11. The clerk's note indicates that Lincoln submitted Mitchell's petition, dated September 6, 1864, to Bates on September 9. See "Register of Letters Received March 2, 1861 – December 31, 1868," Vol. 2 in NARA, Records of the Attorney General's Office, RG 60.

12. Mitchell to Lincoln, October 20, 1864, Lincoln Papers, Library of Congress.

13. Bates to Lincoln, November 30, 1864, Lincoln Papers, Library of Congress. Bates's distinction between the Wilkinson amendment and other "acts" of Congress suggests he concluded that earlier colonization statutes were still in effect, presumably among them the 1862 rebel land tax bill that Mitchell cited.

14. The Treasury Department finalized this payment sometime after January 1, 1865. Its release probably required an order to the Treasury Department signed by Lincoln. Harlan wrote Lincoln on December 31 asking for his authorization to release Mitchell's account. Mitchell's request stated "that the President alone can fix the rate of compensation and order its payment." The letter contained an order to the Treasury Department for Mitchell's payment from January to June 1864, the salary left blank. Mitchell received his salary for this period in early 1865. See Harlan to Lincoln, December 31, 1864, Lincoln Papers, Library of Congress.

15. Mitchell to Simpson, March 12, 1865, Simpson Papers, Library of Congress.

16. Mitchell to Harlan, May 25, 1865; Harlan to Speed, May 27, 1865; Speed to Harlan, June 2, 1865, Slave Trade and Colonization Records.

17. Mitchell to William H. Seward, September 14, 1865, Seward Papers, Reel 90.

18. "The British Honduras Co, Ltd.," *Shareholders' Guardian,* October 18, 1865; "Negro Emigration Commissioner's Brief," *New York Times,* September 23, 1865; Mitchell, *Brief on Emigration and Colonization.*

19. LeRoy P. Graf and Ralph W. Haskins, eds., *The Papers of Andrew Johnson* (Knoxville: University of Tennessee Press, 1967-2000), 8:161.

20. C. Vann Woodward. "Seeds of Failure in Radical Race Policy," *Proceedings of the American Philosophical Society,* 110-11 (1966): 1-9.

21. Mitchell to Harlan, February 8, 1866, Slave Trade and Colonization Records; Harlan to Mitchell, February 10, 1866, in *Senate Executive Documents,* No. 55, Serial 1238, 39th Congress, 1st Session, 64.

22. Menard was apparently found with pamphleteer Samuel Clarke when the latter was arrested. Clarke, a relative of Bogle by marriage, was among those executed by Eyre's controversial order. See "No. 13, Colonies, Jamaica" in *Accounts and Papers of the House of Commons,* Session 1866. 51:229-31; "Memorandum of the late Insurrection in St. Thomas-in-the-East" in *Papers Laid Before the Royal Commission of Inquiry by Governor Eyre* (London: George Edward Eyre and William Spottiswoode, 1866), 76; Adams to Stanley, December 27, 1866, and Stanley to Adams, July 1, 1867, in *Papers Relating to Foreign Affairs* (Washington, D.C.: Government Printing Office, 1868), 114-15; "Death of Mr. J.W. Menard," Kingston *Daily Gleaner,* October 26, 1893.

23. Joan R. Sherman, ed., *African-American Poetry in the Nineteenth Century* (Champaign: University of Illinois Press, 1992), 282.

24. In the same address Menard expressed his frustrations with the Republican Party. He declared "no interest in any movement whose aim is to fire the Northern heart against the South not in the interest of the negro nor of the public welfare, but purely for political power" ("A Negro's View of His Race," *Daily Nevada State Journal,* January 12, 1878).

25. Mary Edward Mitchell, *Memoirs of James Mitchell: Statesman, Educator, Minister* (Mt. Zion, GA: Mt. Zion Seminary, 1939), 11.

26. Marvin R. Cain, *Lincoln's Attorney General: Edward Bates of Missouri.* (Ann Arbor: University of Michigan Press, 1965), 325. See also Bates to James R. Doolittle, October 30, 1865, in "Letters of Edward Bates and the Blairs, from the Private Papers of Senator Doolittle," *Missouri Historical Review,* 11, No. 2 (1917), 127.

27. Mitchell to Grant, February 16, 1871, Slave Trade and Colonization Records. Early versions of the Freedmen's Bureau bill contained provisions putting colonization under the bureau's charge in the War Department, lending some credibility to Mitchell's claims. Colonization was dropped from the final measure though, which passed on March 3, 1865.

28. *Ibid.*

29. The letter from Sumner, dated July 5, 1871, and a synopsis of Mitchell's answer were published in 1894 along with a letter from Mitchell on U.S. expansionism. See "The Western Question," *Atlanta Constitution,* March 25, 1894.

30. M. E. Mitchell, *Memoirs of James Mitchell,* 14-16.

31. "Last Will of James Mitchell," filed March 3, 1903, Judge of Probate Records, Carroll County Courthouse, Carrollton, Georgia.

32. James Mitchell (interview), "Lincoln and the Negro," *St. Louis Daily Globe-Democrat,* August 26, 1894; "Dr. James Mitchell Dead," *Washington Post,* March 3, 1903. Evidence of Mitchell's personal papers and diary may be found in a short biography written by his great-niece Mary Edward Mitchell (born ca. 1885) at the time of his death in 1903. The biography was republished as a small pamphlet by the Mt. Zion Seminary in the late 1930s when it joined Carroll County public school district as Mt. Zion High School. See M. E. Mitchell, *Memoirs of James Mitchell.* The colonization "state papers" in Mitchell's will passed to James Robert Mitchell (born ca. 1861), his nephew and executor. Their present whereabouts are unknown.

CHAPTER 10
COLONIZATION REPUDIATED, COLONIZATION REVIVED?

1. Mitchell to Lincoln, June 1864, Lincoln Papers, Library of Congress.

2. "Mr. Blair's Speech," *Chicago Tribune,* February 10, 1864.

3. For example, see Eric Foner, *Our Lincoln: New Perspectives on Lincoln and His World* (New York, NY: W.W. Norton, 2008), 162-63.

4. Michael Burlingame, ed., *An Oral History of Abraham Lincoln: John G. Nicolay's Interviews and Essays* (Carbondale and Edwardsville: Southern Illinois University Press, 1996), 78.

5. "Judge Blair's Speech," *New York Times,* October 17, 1863.

6. Wilson to Lincoln, August 21, 1863, Lincoln Papers, Library of Congress. Echoing this complaint, Wilson used the occasion of the colonization fund's repeal in 1864 to reiterate his attacks on Blair, *Congressional Globe*, 38th Congress, 1st Session, 3262; Noah Brooks, Michael Burlingame, ed., *Lincoln Observed: The Civil War Dispatches of Noah Brooks* (Baltimore, MD: The Johns Hopkins University Press, 1998), 78-79.

7. "Mr. Blair's Speech," *Chicago Tribune,* February 10, 1864; *Congressional Globe,* 38th Congress, 1st Session, 509-14.

8. Montgomery Blair to Lincoln, February 16, 1864, Lincoln Papers, Library of Congress.

9. Davis to Augustus W. Bradford, January 25, 1864, excerpted in Gerald S. Henig, *Henry Winter Davis* (New York, NY: Twayne Publishers, 1973), 196.

10. Henry Winter Davis, "The Disposition of Freed Negroes," February 25, 1864, *Appendix to the Congressional Globe,* 38th Congress, 1st Session, 45.

11. "From Washington," *Chicago Tribune,* February 26, 1864. The speech was reprinted in a pamphlet entitled "Hon. H. Winter Davis, of Maryland, on the President's Colonization and Compensation Scheme" (Washington, D.C.: L. Towers & Co, 1864). Davis to Du Pont, February 29, 1864, quoted in Henig, *Henry Winter Davis,* 198.

12. Francis P. Blair, Jr., *The Jacobins of Missouri and Maryland* (Washington, D.C.: Francis P. Blair, 1864), 6.

13. C. M. Hawley to Lincoln, February 27, 1864, Lincoln Papers, Library of Congress.

14. William E. Parrish, *Frank Blair, Lincoln's Conservative* (Columbia: University of Missouri Press, 1998), 194.

15. Gideon Welles, "Administration of Abraham Lincoln," *Galaxy* 24, no. 4, (1877): 439.

16. Henry Clay Whitney, *Life on the Circuit with Lincoln* (Boston: Estes & Lauriat, 1892), 4.

17. Welles, "Administration of Abraham Lincoln," 444; Allen Thorndike Rice, ed., *Reminiscences of Abraham Lincoln by Distinguished Men of His Time* (New York: North American Publishing, 1886), 61–62.

18. Pomeroy sided with Usher during the feud over the Emigration Office. During the 1889 event he spoke of his own involvement in the Chiriquí project, which Mitchell eventually came to regard as a competitor to the programs in British Honduras and Guiana. Pomeroy attributed his difficulty in moving colonists to Seward's opposition, though it was likely as much a product of the budget politics surrounding the scheme. "On the day the proclamation was issued…I had 10,000 negroes ready to sail, but Seward stopped us" ("New Stories of Lincoln," *Washington Post,* April 14, 1889).

19. Rice, *Reminiscences of Abraham Lincoln,* 150; Benjamin F. Butler, *Autobiography and Personal Reminiscences of Major-General Benjamin F. Butler* (Boston: A. M. Thayer, 1892), 903 (hereafter cited as *Butler's Book*).

20. Butler, *Butler's Book*, 903.

21. "A Chat about New Books," *Catholic World,* 44, 261:407; "Of General Ben Butler's New Book," *Atlanta Constitution,* March 12, 1891.

22. In one bizarre case from the early twentieth century, Butler's colonization anecdote inadvertently supplied fodder for a notorious attempt to posthumously enlist Lincoln in the prohibition movement. Starting in 1904, an elderly minister named James B. Merwin produced a succession of increasingly fanciful

tales wherein he allegedly conversed with Lincoln about alcohol and temperance. Merwin's actual connection to Lincoln was minimal, consisting of only an army chaplain's commission he received from the president during the Civil War. He nonetheless purported to have visited Lincoln on the morning of the assassination to discuss temperance policies. Merwin also claimed that he was asked by Lincoln to deliver a memorandum about Butler's proposed canal project to Philadelphia newspaperman Alexander McClure. The story was one of Merwin's many fabrications, though it also illustrates the familiarity that Butler's anecdote had attained by this time. See Richard F. Hamm, "The Prohibitionists' Lincoln," *Illinois Historical Journal,* 86 (Summer 1993), 104.

23. Butler's story was readily accepted by several early historians. See Wesley, "Lincoln's Plan," 20; Dunning, *Studies in Southern History,* 28-29; William Eleroy Curtis, *Abraham Lincoln* (Philadelphia, PA: J. P. Lippincott, 1902), 334; Edward McMahon, "Lincoln the Emancipator," *Pacific Historical Review,* 5, 1 (1936): 24; Hans Trefousse, *Ben Butler: The South Called Him Beast!* (New York, NY: Twayne Publishers, 1957), 179. The anecdote also received early acceptance, and even occasional praise, in the black community. The *Chicago Defender* posited that "with the [Panama Canal] colonization project perhaps by this time we could boast of a country or at least a breathing spot we could call our own." See "Lincoln and the Panama Canal," *Chicago Defender,* April 12, 1913. Butler's reliability was apparently the subject of a 1951 letter from Warren Beck to Paul Scheips, two of the first historians to explore the details of the Chiriquí and Île à Vache projects. Beck remarked that Butler's story "ran counter to the established scholarly opinion on the subject," a view that was apparently shared by noted Lincoln scholar Roy P. Basler (Scheips, "Lincoln and Chiriqui," 449, note 57).

24. Mark E. Neely, Jr., "Abraham Lincoln and Black Colonization: Benjamin Butler's Spurious Testimony," *Civil War History* 25 (1979): 77–83.

25. Phillip W. Magness, "Benjamin Butler's Colonization Testimony Reevaluated," *Journal of the Abraham Lincoln Association* 29-1 (2008): 1-28; John Hay to Benjamin F. Butler, April 10, 1865, Benjamin F. Butler Papers, Library of Congress. Butler's meeting with the president was noticed by at least one newspaper. "General Butler was in Washington on Tuesday, consulting with President Lincoln" (*Republican Compiler,* April 17, 1865).

26. It may be of some interest to the present inquiry that Butler's 1886 version of the anecdote makes an apparent reference to the project in British Guiana. Butler notes that Lincoln "attempted to make some provision at Demerara, through the agency of Senator Pomeroy, for colonizing the negroes" sometime prior to the meeting (Rice, *Reminiscences of Abraham Lincoln,* 150).

27. "Spain to Abandon Cuba," *New York Times,* August 20, 1884. Surprisingly, this version of the Butler story appears to have entirely escaped the attention of all historians who have written about the episode until the present day.

28. Michael Vorenberg, a leading critic of the Butler anecdote, has nonetheless speculated about the possibility of its accuracy. "After all, might it be possible…that Butler remembered the date wrong, that Butler told Lincoln his various schemes for

using African soldiers abroad, and Lincoln nodded approvingly, perhaps because he liked the idea or more likely because he wanted to end the conversation with a general whom he did not much like?" (Vorenberg, "Slavery Reparations in Theory and Practice: Lincoln's Approach," in Brian Dirck, ed., *Lincoln Emancipated* [DeKalb: Northern Illinois University Press, 2007], 120).

29. For an extended discussion of the strengths and weaknesses of Butler's anecdote see Magness, "Butler's Colonization Testimony," 26-28.

30. Henry Louis Gates, Jr., *Lincoln on Race and Slavery,* (Princeton, NJ: Princeton University Press, 2009), lviii.

31. Welles, "Administration of Abraham Lincoln," 440, 444.

32. Grant, who was still serving in the military at the time, indicates that his comments on Panama "were a private note," "written without consultation with the Sec. of War whos [*sic*] approval would be necessary in case any such use was made of the Military forces of this country as are here mentioned" (Grant to Seward, November 10, 1865, in John Y. Simon, editor, *The Papers of Ulysses S. Grant* [Carbondale, IL: Southern Illinois University Press, 1988], 15:413).

33. "Last Public Address," Roy P. Basler et al., eds., *Collected Works of Abraham Lincoln*, 9 vols. (New Brunswick, N.J.: Rutgers University Press, 1953–1955), 8:403; Neely, "Lincoln and Black Colonization," 82; Boritt, *The Lincoln Enigma* (Oxford: Oxford University Press, 2002), 18.

34. Gates, *Lincoln on Race,* liv.

35. *Ibid.,* lv, lix; Welles, "Administration of Abraham Lincoln."

36. Kevin R. C. Gutzman, "Abraham Lincoln, Jeffersonian: the Colonization Chimera," in Dirck, ed., *Lincoln Emancipated,* 72.

37. George M. Fredrickson, *Big Enough to Be Inconsistent: Abraham Lincoln Confronts Slavery and Race* (Cambridge, MA: Harvard University Press, 2008), 117-18.

38. Welles, "Administration of Abraham Lincoln," 444.

39. Lincoln had made a strikingly similar comment to Representative William P. Cutler of Ohio some two years prior. After expressing his concern about "the treatment the negroes would receive from the rebels if captured," the president "added that he was troubled to know what we should do with these people – the negroes – after peace came" (February 9, 1863, Diary of William Parker Cutler, in Julia Perkins Cutler, ed., *The Life and Times of Ephraim Cutler* [Cincinnati: Robert Clarke & Co, 1890], 303).

40. For a brief account of the frequently overlooked Cox scheme, see Wilbert H. Ahern, "The Cox Plan of Reconstruction: A Case Study in Ideology and Race Relations," *Civil War History,* 16 (December 1970): 293-308.

CHAPTER 11
COLONIZATION AFTER EMANCIPATION

1. George Fredrickson, "A Man but Not a Brother: Abraham Lincoln and Racial Equality," *Journal of Southern History* 41 (1975): 56–57.

2. For press notice of Hodge's visit see "From Washington," *Chicago Tribune,* April 25, 1863; "Colonization of the Blacks," *New York Times,* May 18, 1863; "Washington," *Presbyterian Banner,* June 17, 1863; "Honduras and Hayti," *The African Repository* (Washington, D. C.: William H. Moore), 39:344.

3. Perhaps overshadowing this question is that of the influence of Henry Clay on Lincoln. The president's words of praise for the Great Compromiser are well known and do not need repetition, but Clay was arguably a less formative figure than historians tend to assume. Certainly it made good political sense for a Republican hopeful to place himself in the mold of the preeminent Whig whatever his private thoughts, while Marvin R. Cain recounted positive examples of Lincoln's cooler feelings on Clay in "Lincoln's Views of Slavery and the Negro: A Suggestion," *Historian*, 26 (1964): 502-20. Though we can never get into Lincoln's mind at this level, this is no insignificant point if Lincoln had indeed added his own spin on colonization and moved significantly beyond a narrower, antebellum conception to a more nuanced one which was more adaptable to the developments of the Civil War.

4. Henry Louis Gates, Jr., *Lincoln on Race and Slavery* (Princeton, NJ: Princeton University Press, 2009), xx.

5. Eric Foner, *Our Lincoln: New Perspectives on Lincoln and His World* (New York, NY: W. W. Norton, 2008), 137.

6. Mark E. Neely, Jr., "Colonization and the Myth That Lincoln Prepared the People for Emancipation," in William A. Blair and Karen Fisher Young, eds., *Lincoln's Proclamation: Emancipation Reconsidered* (Chapel Hill, University of North Carolina Press, 2009), 45-74.

7. While an immediate cause may be found in the budgetary dispute at the Interior Department, the authors would be remiss not to note the lingering mysteries behind the decision of the British Foreign Office to cancel the British Honduras port proclamation in December 1863. Though its details are lost amidst sporadic and incomplete colonial records, word of this order appears to have arrived just as preparations were under way to send the first ship of emigrants from New York. In this event it may be assumed that the resultant delays weakened Mitchell's political position during the budgetary battles of early 1864 by leaving him with a colony that still only existed on paper despite Hodge's apparent readiness to move forward.

8. For an insightful and pertinent exploration of prevailing contemporary ideas of citizenship, community, and racial inclusion, see Michael Vorenberg, "Abraham Lincoln's "Fellow Citizens" - Before and After Emancipation," in Blair and Younger, eds., *Lincoln's Proclamation*, 151-69.

9. One of the authors has researched the Chiriquí project in the private papers of some of the participants for a forthcoming manuscript. The records suggest that its demise was more drawn out and a little more complicated than usually assumed. Most interestingly, there is some evidence that Lincoln contemplated reviving Chiriquí in early January 1863 after he had temporarily suspended the Vache contract.

10. Paul D. Escott, *"What Shall We Do with the Negro?": Lincoln, White Racism, and Civil War America* (Charlottesville: University of Virginia Press, 2009), 218.

Sources

PERSONAL PAPERS

Benjamin F. Butler Papers, Library of Congress, Washington, District of Columbia

Abraham Lincoln Papers, Library of Congress

James Morrison MacKye Papers, Library of Congress

James Shepherd Pike Papers, Library of Congress

William Henry Seward Papers, University of Rochester, Rochester, New York

Matthew Simpson Papers, Library of Congress

Ambrose W. Thompson Papers, Library of Congress

John Palmer Usher Papers, Kansas State Historical Society, Topeka, Kansas

NATIONAL ARCHIVES OF THE UNITED KINGDOM, KEW, RICHMOND, SURREY

Colonial Office Records (CO)

Foreign Office Records (FO)

Public Records Office (PRO)

NATIONAL ARCHIVES AND RECORDS ADMINISTRATION, UNITED STATES, COLLEGE PARK, MARYLAND

Despatches from U.S. Consuls in Georgetown, Demerara, British Guiana (RG 59, T 336)

Despatches from U.S. Consuls in Belize, British Honduras (RG 59, T 334)

Despatches from United States Ministers in the Netherlands (RG 59, M 42)

Diplomatic Instructions of the Department of State: the Netherlands (RG 59, M 77)
Miscellaneous Letters of the Department of State (RG 59, M 179)
Notes from the Dutch Legation (RG 59, T 5)
Notes to Foreign Legations in the United States from the Department of State: the Netherlands (RG 59, M 99)
Records of the Attorney General's Office (RG 60)
Records of Foreign Service Posts: Consular Posts: Paramaribo (RG 84)
Records of Foreign Service Posts: Diplomatic Posts: the Netherlands (RG 84)
Records of the United States Department of the Interior, relating to the Suppression of the African Slave Trade and Negro Colonization (RG 48, M 160)
Treasury Solicitor Records (TS)

OTHER RECORDS

American Freedmen's Inquiry Commission Papers, Houghton Library, Harvard University, Cambridge, Massachusetts
Judge of Probate Records, Carroll County Courthouse, Carrollton, Georgia

Index

About the Authors

Phillip W. Magness obtained his MPP and Ph.D. from George Mason University in Fairfax, Virginia, specializing in policy history. Outside of his historical writing, Magness has worked on academic and research programs for the Institute for Humane Studies at George Mason University. He is Visiting Assistant Professor of Economics at the Campbell School of Business at Berry College in Mount Berry, Georgia.

Sebastian N. Page received both his undergraduate and postgraduate education at the University of Oxford. He is a historian of the period that spans the American Revolution through the Civil War, with a particular interest in the latter. A current project is a focused study of black colonization as policy during the Civil War. He is a junior research fellow at the Queen's College, Oxford.